Thatcherism

Short Histories

Agenda Short Histories are incisive and provocative introductions to topics, ideas and events for students wanting to know more about how we got where we are today.

Published

Conservatism
Mark Garnett

Thatcherism
Peter Dorey

Thatcherism

Peter Dorey

agenda
publishing

First published in 2023 by Agenda Publishing

Agenda Publishing Limited
PO Box 185
Newcastle upon Tyne
NE20 2DH
www.agendapub.com

ISBN 978-1-78821-547-3 (hardcover)
ISBN 978-1-78821-548-0 (paperback)

British Library Cataloguing-in-Publication Data
A catalogue record for this book is available from the British Library

Typeset by JS Typesetting Ltd, Porthcawl, Mid Glamorgan
Printed and bound in the UK by TJ Books

Contents

Preface

Ten years after Margaret Thatcher's death, and with her free-market or neoliberal philosophy seemingly beset by increasing conflicts and contradictions, and therefore subject to growing criticism, this is a timely opportunity to revisit her eponymous ideology. In this short book, the key concepts, objectives and policies of Thatcherism are examined, in tandem with the intellectual sources, arguments and discourse which shaped and underpinned it. The book also considers how Thatcher and her ideological adherents exercised a dominance in the Conservative Party far greater than their actual numerical strength in the 1980s, and the extent to which Thatcherism subsequently became hegemonic in the Conservative Party, particularly in terms of the continued, indeed, intensified, commitment to free-market economics, low direct taxation, privatization, deregulation, "marketization" of public services, reduced workers' rights and employment protection to promote labour market flexibility and restore managerial authority in the workplace, and relentless attempts to reduce welfare expenditure and entitlement. So entrenched has economic neoliberalism become in the Conservative Party, that almost any problems in the British economy and society are interpreted as evidence that the Thatcherite revolution is still incomplete.

In an additional chapter, we examine some of the contradictions or unintended consequences of Thatcherism that have become increasingly evident since the 1980s. These include the manner in which the 1986 deregulation of financial services ushered in an era of unprecedented consumer borrowing and spending, which was totally at odds with Thatcher's own moral strictures about personal frugality, self-restraint and thrift; the new modes and layers of regulatory bureaucracy yielded by privatization and "marketization" of public services like education and healthcare, in spite of Thatcherite denigration of red tape and state interference; the manner in which the transformation of universities into businesses, and students into fee-paying customers, has led to a proliferation of degrees in subjects which the Conservative right view with deep disdain and disapproval, but which universities find profitable because many students (as sovereign consumers) wish to study them; the general weakening of values and virtues which Conservatives have traditionally revered and defended – community, continuity, deference, family life, organic society, reciprocal duties and responsibilities, social harmony and stability – these having been grievously undermined by the Thatcherite veneration of acquisitive individualism, change/modernization, competition, consumerism, the negative impact on families of longer or more unsocial working hours and/or unaffordable housing, and short-termism (in the economic sphere) as companies seek to increase profits or share-holder value as quickly as possible, rather than adopting a longer-term stance. This has greatly increased job insecurity and precarity among the working class and middle class alike, along with a relentless intensification of the labour process and micro-management of workers via target-setting, monitoring and performance measurement.

This book is also timely because of the relatively recent publication or release of archival and other primary sources that offer new insights into the Thatcher premiership. The Thatcher Foundation (TF) itself has proved a veritable goldmine of original material, such as correspondence – often with Thatcher's own hand-written comments and sometimes acerbic remarks – between key figures (such as Thatcher herself, of course, John Hoskyns, Keith Joseph, Ferdinand Mount, Alfred Sherman, Norman Strauss and Alan Walters), draft policy proposals and speeches, whereas ministerial papers pertaining to the latter part of the Thatcher premiership have only relatively recently been released by the National Archives (NA), although the erstwhile 30-year rule has now become a 20-year rule. This book has also consulted the many autobiographies, diaries and memoirs published in the last ten years by some of Thatcher's former colleagues, such as Kenneth Clarke, Oliver Letwin, Chris Patten, Malcolm Rifkind, Caroline Slocock and David Waddington.

In writing this book, and making use of these new(er) sources, I have gained fresh insights and a deeper understanding of Thatcherism. I very much hope that readers will benefit similarly.

Pete Dorey
Bath, Somerset

1

Why Margaret Thatcher became Conservative Party leader and prime minister

When Margaret Thatcher became Conservative leader in February 1975, she had not yet fully embraced the principles and policies which were subsequently developed into Thatcherism. However, she instinctively perceived that the path chosen by the postwar Conservative Party had been a mistake, and her experiences as a minister in Edward Heath's 1970–74 cabinet reinforced her growing conviction – fully shared by Keith Joseph – that the Conservatives needed a change of ideological direction. At this stage, however, her instinctive ideas and philosophy were not fully formed, so that at the time of the Conservative leadership contest, Thatcher had only recently embarked upon her process of political reappraisal and search for a new mode of Conservatism.

It has been widely believed that in the 1975 Conservative leadership contest, many Conservative MPs voted for Thatcher primarily because they were determined to replace Heath, and most of the other leadership contenders were his allies or associates: "Electing Margaret had simply been the most effective way of getting rid of Ted" (Critchley & Halcrow 1998: 60; see also Riddell 1985: 10). However, although she undoubtedly attracted support from many Conservative MPs by virtue of not being Heath, this has been exaggerated as the main motive for voting for her, and therefore underestimated the extent to which Thatcher genuinely appealed to some Conservative MPs in her own right, either due to her apparent personal qualities or/and her nascent right-wing views. After all, if Conservative MPs had merely wanted a new leader whose most important characteristic was that they were "not Heath", there were others in the second ballot, such as William Whitelaw and James Prior, who were associated with him ideologically, but were potentially more politically attractive. It therefore behoves us to examine more carefully, and with more nuance, how and why Thatcher was elected Conservative leader in early 1975.

Three discrete factors need to be considered: the unavailability of other candidates representing the Conservative right; the manner in which Thatcher was already beginning to develop a distinct ideological stance and policy agenda, even though it did not yet warrant the soubriquet Thatcherism; the extent to which she had impressed some Conservative MPs with her parliamentary performance as a shadow Treasury minister since the previous year's election defeats.

Thatcher as the "stalking horse" candidate of the Conservative right

In the 1975 Conservative leadership contest, there were few contenders representing the party's right, not least because Enoch Powell, an ultra-neoliberal (long before the term was used) and anti-European Community (EC), anti-immigration, English nationalist, had defected to the Ulster Unionists in the 1974 general elections, due to fundamental disagreements with key aspects of Conservative policy. This obviously precluded Powell from standing as a candidate in the subsequent Conservative leadership contest, but had he still been eligible, he would almost certainly have been immensely popular with the party's right, not only because of his staunch economic liberalism, defence of parliamentary sovereignty and eloquence as a public speaker, but because his 1968 (anti-immigration) "rivers of blood" speech had immediately raised both his public profile, and his popularity with sections of England's working class (not dissimilar to Nigel Farage's more recent proletarian appeal).

The other potential candidate whose developing neoliberalism might have garnered support from the Conservative right was Keith Joseph, but he declined to offer himself as a candidate following a poorly-received speech in which he had claimed that: "The balance of our population, our human stock is threatened ... [because] ... a high and rising proportion of children are being born to mothers least fitted to bring children into the world and to bring them up". He claimed that these overwhelmingly destitute, working-class mothers, often unmarried and still in their late teens, "are producing problem children, the future unmarried mothers, delinquents, denizens of our borstals, subnormal educational establishments, prisons and hostels for drifters" (quoted in *The Times*, 21 October 1974). The controversy aroused by the speech, and the implication that he was dabbling in eugenics, led Joseph to concede that, although he had apparently been misunderstood or misrepresented, he had also been unwise in his choice of words, and that he lacked the tact or diplomatic skills needed to be a successful party leader and potential prime minister.

With Powell and Joseph both ruled out of contention, Thatcher offered herself as a leadership contender instead. Although she was not yet a fully-fledged Thatcherite, she did view herself as a candidate who could appeal to the Tory right, because she only announced her challenge after another senior Conservative, Edward Du Cann, had declined to put himself forward as a contender. Hitherto, Thatcher had refrained, insisting that: "We must not split the right-wing vote". Yet even then, Thatcher did not consider herself a serious contender, confessing that "it seemed to me most unlikely that I would win. But I did think that by entering the race, I would draw in other stronger candidates" (Thatcher 1995: 267). Many of the Conservatives' old guard seriously underestimated Thatcher, with the veteran One Nation Tory from the 1950s and 1960s, Rab Butler, asking Chris Patten (at the Conservative Research Department): "We don't have to take this Thatcher business seriously, do we?" (Patten 2009: 83).

Certainly, there was a widespread expectation that if the contest proceeded to a second ballot, due to Heath not winning the first, then more serious or senior candidates would offer themselves, having not stood initially out of loyalty to Heath (Campbell 2015: 321). Nonetheless, when Joseph informed Thatcher that he was not going to stand, due to the controversy over his "eugenics" speech, Thatcher resolved that: "We just could not abandon the Party and the country to Ted's brand of politics … someone who represents our viewpoint *has* to stand" (Thatcher 1995: 266, emphasis in original).

Some of the Conservative MPs who supported Thatcher in the first ballot did so tactically, intending to ensure Heath's defeat and elimination from the contest, whereupon more credible or senior candidates would offer themselves in the second ballot. In fact, Thatcher herself envisaged this scenario, anticipating that "a substantial number of those voting for me in the first round would only do so as a tactical way of removing Ted, and putting in someone more acceptable but still close to his way of thinking" (Thatcher 1995: 278). Certainly, Nigel Fisher confessed that he was one of those several Conservative MPs who voted for Thatcher in the first ballot, but without necessarily intending to vote for her in a second ballot: "I wanted to see what other candidates might enter the lists at that stage before committing myself" (Fisher 1977: 163)

There were even some Conservative MPs whose prime motive in voting for Thatcher was to send a warning to Heath to become a more collective or collegial leader, the rationale being that ostensibly supporting Thatcher would reduce Heath's widely anticipated lead in the contest, thereby persuading him to change his leadership style. As one Conservative insider recalled, Thatcher received a few votes from "Heathites" who "wanted to teach him a lesson, to make sure that he would be more responsive to their concerns in the future". Overconfident of Heath's imminent victory, and thus fatally underestimating Thatcher's prospects, such MPs assumed that they could vote for the latter in order to reduce Heath's margin of victory. These MPs were also encouraged in their complacency by Thatcher's campaign manager, Airey Neave, who cunningly "downplayed the support she was actually receiving", so that Conservative MPs who simply wanted Heath re-elected without a landslide were persuaded that this could best be achieved by voting for Thatcher; if she had no chance of winning, as they assumed or were led to believe, then it would be safe to vote for her in order to chasten Heath (Ranelagh 1992: 144).

There was thus considerable surprise when Thatcher polled the most votes in the first ballot on 4 February 1975, attracting the support of 130 Conservative MPs compared to the 119 who remained loyal to Heath, with the rank outsider Hugh Fraser mustering just 16 votes. At that time, the Conservative Party's rules stipulated that a leadership contender had to secure not just a majority of votes, but a lead of at least 15 per cent. Technically, therefore, Thatcher had not achieved enough votes to be declared the outright winner, but the scale of her support was sufficient for Heath to acknowledge defeat and resign. He subsequently noted that Thatcher's lead in the first ballot was partly accidental, in that some Conservative MPs had voted for her in the hope of ensuring a second ballot, whereupon a politically more attractive or unity candidate could present themselves. Heath was aggrieved at Neave's tactic of deliberately downplaying Thatcher's support and prospects: "I was told afterwards of the Conservative Members who fell for this cunning manoeuvre". Indeed, Heath was "convinced that I would have won the first ballot if he [Neave] had not taken charge of the Thatcher campaign" (Heath 1998: 532; see also Hurd 2003: 231).

With Heath out of the contest, the second ballot heralded four new contestants alongside Thatcher; John Peyton and Geoffrey Howe associated with the party's right, and James Prior and William Whitelaw as the supposedly Heathite or continuity candidates. Thatcher herself was somewhat unnerved by Howe's candidature, "because he held similar views to mine and might split the right-wing vote", thereby making it much more likely that a Heathite candidate would secure a majority (Thatcher 1995: 278). Yet by this stage, Thatcher had established momentum and further raised her profile and credibility, sufficient to win by a clear majority:

Margaret Thatcher	146
William Whitelaw	79
James Prior	19
Sir Geoffrey Howe	19
John Peyton	11

From the outset, her election as Conservative leader caused concern in parts of the party, although some of this was clearly derived from sexism and classism. Some non-Thatcherite Conservatives feared that she symbolized a narrowing of the party's outlook and views, and this would alienate middle-of-the-road voters. For example, Norman Fowler "shared the view of many of my contemporaries that Margaret Thatcher presented the wrong image as far as the party was concerned, and that we would suffer gravely if we appeared to leave the centre ground of politics" (Fowler 1991: 15). According to Julian Critchley, one of her most trenchant, but wittiest, backbench critics, Thatcher's rise reflected "a process of petit-embourgeoisement" which "served to narrow the horizons of the Party" (Critchley 1978: 467; see also Burton-Cartledge 2021: 49–50; Meyer 1990: 179; Montgomery-Massingberd 1986: 22). Similarly, in spite of being a wealthy self-made entrepreneur – precisely the type of person that Thatcher normally admired immensely – Michael Heseltine was concerned from the outset that she emanated "from a certain social background, one step up the ladder of economic success, with it a lot of the characteristics that you associate with people who have just made it, a certain intolerance of those who haven't, a certain suspicion of those who are further up the ladder, a certain bigotry, slightly over-simplistic solutions about the nature of the society in which they live" (BBC2 2019a).

Elsewhere, Byron Criddle (1994: 161) argued that Thatcher's election reflected and reinforced a wider and deeper change in the Conservative Party, namely "the switch … from the shires to the suburbs: from estate owners to estate agents". Such concerns would have been compounded as Thatcher's ideas and policy preferences crystallized, and it became evident that she sought a new political direction for the Conservative Party. On the other hand, this is exactly what some Conservative MPs wanted too, having grown similarly disillusioned with the party's ideological direction of travel since 1945.

Thatcher's developing ideological shift and emerging policy agenda

The philosophy and policies which subsequently constituted the political doctrine of Thatcherism were already being developed in the wake of the downfall of the 1970–74 Heath government, and the disillusionment that Thatcher and Joseph both felt having served as ministers. We discuss the origins and development of Thatcher's political philosophy, and the role of key figures such as Friedrich Hayek, Joseph himself, and Alfred Sherman, in the next chapter, but it is important to acknowledge here that, to those who paid close attention at the time of the 1975 Conservative leadership contest, Thatcher was already articulating a somewhat more right-wing perspective, and thus rejecting many of the interventionist and neo-corporatist policies which the Heath administration had recently pursued.

This is crucial to understanding some of Thatcher's support among Conservative MPs in February 1975 and provides a corrective to the common (but erroneous) view that her election was due simply to her not being Edward Heath. Had enough Conservative MPs wanted Heathism without Heath, they could have supported James Prior or William Whitelaw in the second ballot, so Thatcher's victory clearly suggests that her appeal derived from other factors. Evidently, some Conservative MPs discerned that she was, potentially at least, offering something new or different, even though she was only just beginning to develop her counter-ideology. After all, as Norman Tebbit subsequently noted, "there was little point in changing the leader if we were to be stuck with the same policies", while Nicholas Ridley recalled that the Conservative Party "was looking for a change in leadership, a change of style and a change of policies" (Tebbit 1988: 142; Ridley 1991: 10).

As such, claims that Thatcher's 1975 election to the Conservative leadership were primarily or solely due to her not being Edward Heath are simplistic to the point of inaccuracy. While she was not yet a fully-formed Thatcherite, it was already evident that she was crafting a different mode of Conservatism to that which had prevailed since 1945, and that while this worried One Nation Tories, some disillusioned Conservative MPs welcomed the nascent change of direction (Cowley & Bailey 2000; Stacey 2021; Wickham-Jones 1997).

That Thatcher wanted to pursue a different type of Conservatism had become apparent from the talks she gave to some Conservative MPs during her leadership campaign, sundry media interviews, and an article she penned in *The Daily Telegraph* on 30 January. In the latter, titled "My Kind of Tory Party", Thatcher rebutted allegations, both from critics inside the Conservative Party and from the left generally, that her nascent mode of Conservatism would only appeal to the provincial middle class, rather than all sections of British society. In meeting this criticism head-on, she declared that,

> ... if "middle class values" include the encouragement of variety and individual choice, the provision of fair incentives and rewards for skill and hard work, the maintenance of effective barriers against the excessive power of the state and a belief in the wide distribution of individual private property, then they are certainly what I am trying to defend ... Sneering at "middle-class values" is to insult the working class no less than the bourgeois. Do British workers have no deep feelings for freedom, for order, for the education of their children, for the right to work without disruption by political militants? Of course they do. And if they are no more than cash-grabbing anarchists, then we must all bear some of the responsibility and try to show them the way back to sanity. But I do not believe they are. Most of them want to do a fair day's work in a job that gives them satisfaction – and strongly resent what they regard

as state subsidies to shirkers. Most of them deplore violence, truancy and indiscipline in schools … My kind of Tory party would make no secret of its belief in individual freedom and individual prosperity, in the maintenance of law and order, in the wide distribution of private property, in rewards for energy, skill and thrift, in diversity of choice, in the preservation of local rights in local communities. (Thatcher 1975)

We discuss in the next chapter the ideas and intellectual sources which collectively and cumulatively constituted Thatcherism, and thereby provided a paradigm shift in British politics during the 1980s and beyond.

Her impressive parliamentary performances from the opposition frontbench

Some of Thatcher's support in the 1975 leadership contest derived from her energy and enthusiasm, and sheer force of personality, attributes which proved attractive to many Conservative MPs, especially those who had found Heath's style of leadership and personality stilted and wooden to the point of brusqueness (Norton 1978: 228–30; see also Campbell 1993: 103; Fisher 1977: 132–3; Patten 2018: 232; Renton 2004: 296). However, this was a double-edged sword, because her outward confidence, and increasingly combative style of leadership, irked some Conservatives, partly because of the ideological convictions which underpinned her political approach and public pronouncements, but also, in some cases, due to pure misogyny and sexism; in this context, a dislike or fear of assertive women, invariably denouncing them as "pushy" or "bossy", pejorative adjectives which they would never have deployed to describe a confident man.

Thatcher had unwittingly been provided with an opportunity to display the combative aspect of her character when Heath, in 1974, appointed her to the shadow Treasury team, which afforded her ample opportunities to attack the Labour government's economic policies, and in particular, the tax increases imposed by the chancellor, Dennis Healey in his first Budget. Had Heath appointed Thatcher to a less prominent post, or one where her political and oratorical skills would have had fewer opportunities to be displayed, it is unlikely that she would have attracted as much support among Conservative MPs in the subsequent leadership contest. Many politicians would struggle to shine or impress in speeches on highly technical or dry issues pertaining to taxation, but in responding to Healey's Budget, Thatcher thrived, and thereupon enormously enhanced her reputation among sections of the parliamentary Conservative Party in the months preceding the 1975 leadership contest. In this regard, Heath had unintentionally awarded Thatcher a frontbench post which enabled her to shine, and thereby garner respect among some Conservative MPs who had previously paid her little attention.

Having studied chemistry as a student, and then trained as a barrister, Thatcher applied her forensic skills to provide a detailed critique of Healey's allegedly punitive taxation policies, thereby alerting Conservative MPs to her intelligence, grasp of detail and confident parliamentary performance: "She marshalled huge quantities of statistics with the strict logic of the lawyer and chemist", which were then articulated with "vigour and certainty of delivery" (Wapshott & Brock 1983: 162). She further endeared herself to some Conservative MPs by her acerbic verbal attacks on Healey: on one notable occasion, after he had ridiculed her in a blatantly patronising manner, Thatcher retorted that: "Some chancellors are macro-economic. Other chancellors are fiscal. This one is just plain cheap" (Hansard 1975, Vol. 884, cols 1553–4). Certainly, some of her speeches denouncing aspects of Healey's Budget endeared her to many Conservative MPs who had not previously viewed her as a possible future party leader. As Cecil Parkinson recalled, "those very strong speeches ... actually did quite a lot to establish her as a potential leader ... turned a lot of people's minds ... it was a big turning point for her" (quoted in Young & Sloman 1986: 31; Ranelagh 1992: 142).

Thatcher's clear grasp of detail, her evident energy and enthusiasm, and her ability to attack her political opponents with both forensic logic, skilful oratory and sometimes barbed retorts, endeared her to some Conservative MPs who were not Thatcherites; they supported Thatcher in the 1975 leadership contest more for her personal qualities, and an expectation that these would prove attractive to many voters, rather than because they wholeheartedly agreed with her nascent ideological stance. In other words, while some Conservative MPs were politically attracted to Thatcher precisely because they shared her developing political views and values, others supported her partly despite her emerging, but clearly more right-wing and combative style of Conservatism. For example, the decidedly non-Thatcherite Malcolm Rifkind recalls that, after voting for Heath in the first ballot, he supported Thatcher in the second vote having been "impressed by her fierce, pugnacious, style. She had a vitality that was not apparent in Whitelaw and the other male candidates" (Rifkind 2016: 129). Of course, her pugnacious style was inextricably linked to her ideological stance, but, in 1975, for some Conservative MPs like Rifkind, it was her personality, and potential leadership qualities, rather than her fledgling ideology, which persuaded them to support Thatcher.

Thatcher's use of ethos and pathos

While developing her counter-ideology in opposition (see Chapter 2), Thatcher was cognizant of the need to convince sceptical Conservative Party members, and potential voters, of her credibility as party leader and, ultimately, future prime minister. Not only would this imbue her leadership with more authority and legitimacy, and enhance her right to be heard, it would also, she envisaged, validate the intellectual paradigm shift and concomitant policy changes that she was increasingly keen to pursue, but for which she realized there was considerable scepticism. To this purpose, Thatcher not only proposed a new approach and policies on ideological grounds, most notably a professed need to replace socialism with capitalism, particularly in response to the serious economic problems engulfing Britain in the latter half of the 1970s, she also sought to justify her prognosis of Britain's plight and proposed remedies by citing her own lower-middle class or petit-bourgeois background and experiences as the daughter of a self-employed shopkeeper in the market town of Grantham, Lincolnshire. As we also note in the next chapter, some of the people who were instrumental in encouraging and strengthening Thatcher's instinctive or nascent ideological views during the opposition years recognized the vital influence of Grantham and her family background on her political outlook and vision.

In citing her family background and early life experiences as the basis of her emerging and eponymous ideology – while also directly citing intellectual influences like Milton Friedman and Friedrich Hayek, depending on who her audience was for any speech – Thatcher deployed two particular techniques familiar to students of political oratory and rhetoric, namely invoking *ethos* and *pathos* (on Thatcher's oratory and rhetoric in general, see Dorey 2015a; Crines, Heppell & Dorey 2016).

Ethos

The deployment of ethos was especially important to Thatcher in the early years of her leadership in order to establish her credibility with the Conservatives' grass-roots membership, and the party's supporters in Britain generally. Many Conservatives, both inside the party and in the country beyond, had been accustomed to leaders who emanated from elite backgrounds in terms of education, kinship, or profession, and who benefited from a high degree of deference, both inside the Conservative Party, and among much of British society, not least sections of the working class. These leaders had also all been men. Although Edward Heath had originated from a modest social and provincial background, his electoral record (one victory out of four) and "unclubbable" personality had led some Conservative MPs to wonder whether the party ought to revert back to its erstwhile patrician leadership, rather than electing another "outsider" to be party leader and potential prime minister.

From the outset, therefore, Thatcher was fully cognizant of the fact that although many Conservative MPs genuinely supported her, and subscribed to her developing mode of radical Conservatism, there was still considerable scepticism in the party at the prospect of being successfully led by a woman from a petit-bourgeois background; in effect, she was initially the victim both of sexism and classism. She was fully aware of this, noting that "in the eyes of the 'wet' Tory establishment, I was not only a woman, but 'that woman', someone not just of a different sex, but of a different class" (Thatcher 1993: 129). She had also not held any of the great offices of state, namely chancellor of the exchequer, foreign secretary and home secretary, and thus fully recognized the urgent need to establish, not only her leadership skills and political acumen, but her right to be heard in the first place and inter alia establish a connection both with Conservative Party members, and key groups of the British electorate, especially the lower-middle class, self-employed, small business proprietors, and the aspirational or skilled working class (the "C2s").

Ironically, whereas pre-Heath Conservative leaders had been admired partly because of their establishment backgrounds and having the "right sort" of personal connections and "old boy" networks, which supposedly rendered them eminently suited to governing and providing political leadership, Thatcher inverted this by assiduously emphasizing her relatively humble socio-economic background, and in so doing, conveyed the message to party members and millions of potential Conservative voters that she was just like them; she was not part of the privileged, public-school-educated, elite which acquired its wealth through inheritance, kinship, marriage, or the old school tie. Instead, Thatcher proudly emphasized the extent to which she emanated from an ordinary family background, worked hard, and succeeded through her own efforts and ambition; the very personification of meritocracy.

For example, in a television documentary during the 1975 Conservative leadership contest, she explained that: "I believe I represent an attitude, an approach, and I believe that that approach is borne out by the development in my own life going to an ordinary state school, having no privileges at all, except perhaps the ones which count most, a good home background with parents who are very interested in their children and interested in getting on, and that's what I see as the kind of conservative approach" (Granada TV 1975). A few months later, in a profile in *The Times* newspaper, Thatcher reiterated the importance of her modest family background and the values her parents had instilled, explaining that:

"My sister and I were brought up in the atmosphere that you work hard to get on. My father and mother set that atmosphere. They both worked very, very hard ... Although you wanted a lot more things in the house, you didn't live beyond your means. They embedded in us very strongly that work and cleanliness were next to godliness ... When you haven't had a good start, self-education counts for much more than the education which you receive at school" (quoted in Connell 1975). On another occasion, appearing on the BBC's *Desert Island Discs*, Thatcher briefly alluded to the impact of her family upbringing, recalling that "it was very hard indeed, but my goodness me, it stood me in good stead" (BBC Radio 4 1978).

Pathos

Another rhetorical device deployed by Thatcher was that of pathos, whereby she endeavoured to strike an emotional chord and connection with her audience, either by expressing sympathy with their problem(s) or plight, or by claiming to have experienced it herself. In instances of the latter, Thatcher often melded ethos and pathos, because she often linked the anxieties or concerns of her audience with her own experiences, thus reaffirming that she was just like them both in terms of personal background and problems previously encountered, and thus political views and values. Thatcher's rhetorical use of pathos was often invoked when eulogizing entrepreneurs, the self-employed and small businesses especially (who constituted much of the Conservatives grass-roots membership and were an important source of electoral support), along with "hard-working families" in general.

Just ten days after being elected Conservative Party leader, Thatcher used a speech in Glasgow to attack the economic policies of the Labour government, claiming that:

> ... in no field has the vindictiveness of Socialist policies been more apparent than in their effect on small business ... the family business has been the backbone of commerce and industry ... We have had the massive increase in rates – with threats of worse to come. We have the savage proposals on state pension contributions for the self-employed – and we warned the electorate in October about this. We have the spitefulness of the Capital Transfer Tax, which strikes at the heart of the family business. (TF 1975a)

Not only did Thatcher explicitly mention small and family businesses, she sought to ingratiate herself further with her audience by use of "we" when referring to the recent increases in rates and pension contributions, and the impact of the capital transfer tax. By using the first-person plural, Thatcher clearly intended to emphasize that she fully shared their anger or frustration, not just ideologically or politically, but because of her own family background as the daughter of a self-employed businessman. Thatcher reiterated her attack on Labour's treatment of small firms in her first leader's speech, at the 1975 Conservative Party conference, when she alleged that: "The Labour government have pursued a disastrous vendetta against small businesses and the self-employed", and pledged that: "We [the Conservatives] will reverse their damaging policies" (TF 1975b).

This use of pathos was reiterated three years later, at the 1978 Conservative Party conference, when Thatcher condemned "Labour's bias against men and women who seek to better themselves and their families. Ordinary people – small businessmen, the self-employed – are not to be allowed to rise on their own. They must rise collectively or not at all" (TF 1978a). A few years later, as prime minister, Thatcher again melded pathos with ethos in her speech to the 1985 Scottish Conservatives' conference. In a passage criticizing the local government rating system, particularly as it applied to businesses, she declared: "I know how commercial ratepayers feel; I spent my early years living above the shop" (TF 1985a).

Thatcher therefore came to symbolize the moral economy of the petite bourgeoisie, whose socio-economic backgrounds, frugal or modest lifestyles, advocacy of hard work, and belief in independence (from the state), inculcated them, as a class, with a strong ethos of individualism and self-reliance, which was *ipso facto* hostile to collectivism, trade unionism, wealth redistribution and welfare dependency (on the moral economy of the petite bourgeoisie, and its political ramifications, see Bechhofer & Elliot 1981). This petite bourgeoisie was also characterized by considerable precarity, as their low profit margins rendered them particularly vulnerable to higher wage claims and/or strikes by trade unions; even if their own staff were not on strike, industrial action by other workers could disrupt their supplies, and impede their ability to continue trading or provide their customers' orders. Unlike bigger firms with correspondingly larger storage facilities or warehouses, and thus a greater ability to continue trading if their supplies of raw materials were temporarily disrupted, small firms and the self-employed were often reliant on daily or weekly deliveries, and therefore much more vulnerable to the disruption or delays accruing from industrial action.

Not surprisingly, much of the petite bourgeoisie is particularly hostile to trade unions and associated industrial action, and thus highly receptive to right-wing pledges to clampdown on "bolshie" workers and trade unions, and thereby restore managerial authority in the workplace. Part of this hostility, however, also derives from a form of envy, because the self-employed or small business owners cannot increase their own incomes by withdrawing their labour, and so understandably resent those who can secure higher incomes by pursuing industrial action, or merely threatening to do so.

Thatcher's initially restrained radicalism

For much of her time as party leader while the Conservatives were in opposition, there was little indication that Thatcher was going to lead them to victory in the next general election, which needed to be held by October 1979 at the latest. Prime ministers enjoyed the constitutional prerogative of formally deciding when to call a general election, provided that it was within five years of the previous one. Certainly, the opinion polls for most of the latter half of the 1970s did not depict any decisive shift in support to the Conservatives. For example, in the spring of 1976, just over a year after Thatcher's election as Conservative leader, Labour enjoyed a 6–7 per cent lead in Ipsos Mori polls, and although the Conservatives did establish a lead for much of 1977 and 1978, it was not clear-cut or consistent: in September 1977, the Conservative lead was 7 per cent, but by May 1978, Labour had a 1 per cent lead. Furthermore, despite the serious economic difficulties facing Britain and the Labour government, James Callaghan was often rated rather more highly as an effective or likeable political leader than Margaret Thatcher: in October 1977, 53 per cent of people were satisfied with Callaghan's leadership of the country compared to 43 per cent who were satisfied with Thatcher's leadership of the Conservative Party. In effect, Callaghan was rather more highly regarded than the government or party he led, and this remained the situation a year or so later – just before the "winter of discontent" – when the corresponding approval ratings for Callaghan and Thatcher were 54 per cent and 38 per cent respectively.

Throughout this period, Thatcher was acutely aware that many of her senior "One Nation" colleagues remained broadly wedded to the moderate or middle-of-the-road consensus politics and policies which had prevailed since 1945. This meant that Thatcher had to proceed carefully, lest the radicalism which she increasingly yearned for either frightened potential Conservative voters who rejected ideology in favour of gradualism, pragmatism and stability, or revealed electorally damaging divisions in the Conservative Party, which would also raise questions about what the party really stood for, and who it ultimately represented or was appealing to. Yet even this caution was insufficient to assuage the concerns of some One Nation Conservative MPs that Thatcher was focusing too much on the provincial middle class and particularly the petite bourgeoisie.

These intra-party divisions ensured that some of the Conservatives' policy stances remained mired in ambiguity during this period, reflecting not just the compromises of managing an increasingly ideologically divided party, but the concern not to frighten those voters who eschewed radicalism. As her official biographer remarked, during this time Thatcher was often "trapped in moderation" (Moore 2013: 363). For example, although Thatcher herself could not conceal her distaste for trade unions, and Norman Tebbit was steadily acquiring his reputation as a "union basher" through some highly critical speeches, the Conservative Party's formal stance on trade union reform was notable for its equivocation, as personified by the caution and emollience of the shadow employment secretary, James Prior. His refusal to promise radical statutory curbs on the trade unions privately frustrated Thatcher, irked Tebbit, and enraged some of her advisers, to the extent that two of the latter, John Hoskyns and Norman Strauss, implored her to sack Prior, arguing that he was a "deadweight of obstruction – very much like the deadweight of the unions in the economy itself" (Hoskyns 2000: 67).

However, Thatcher recognized that, tactically, retaining Prior in this post would reassure voters who might be apprehensive that a Conservative government would provoke class war or industrial conflict by launching an all-out assault on the trade unions. Similarly, Prior's retention would also nullify warnings by the unions themselves that the Conservatives were planning to eviscerate trade unionism and leave workers defenceless against employers and management; such warning could be dismissed as hyperbole and scaremongering, with the implication that it was union leaders who were being extreme and confrontational, not the apparently cautious Conservative leadership.

A similar ambiguity was evinced over incomes policy, on which the One Nation Tories continued to believe that governments needed to specify limits for pay increases each year, preferably through dialogue with trade union leaders, as a key means of curbing inflation. In contrast, Thatcherites, increasingly influenced by Friedman, Hayek, Powell and (Adam) Smith – as we discuss in the next chapter – were becoming convinced that incomes policies were inappropriate, even irrelevant, to curbing inflation, because of the neoliberal premise that it was, ultimately, increases in the money supply, rather than wages, fuelling price increases. Moreover, Thatcherites were opposed to incomes polices because they politicized pay bargaining, which they believed ought to be a purely economic issue (beyond the public sector, of course) determined by market criteria such as supply and demand, the need to recruit and retain staff, affordability, productivity, profitability, and so on, rather than social considerations such as comparability, fairness, justice or tackling poverty.

The ambiguities deriving from these ideological differences, and the need not to alienate potential Conservative voters by appearing too radical – although some on the right feared that the Conservative Party might fail to win enough support by being too timid instead – were evident in much of *The Right Approach to the Economy*, a policy document published in October 1977, and co-authored by Geoffrey Howe, David Howell, Keith Joseph and James Prior. For example, it stated that: "We see the trade unions as a very important economic interest group whose co-operation and understanding we must work constantly to win and to keep, as we have done in the past. We see no need for confrontation and have no wish for it", but added that if politically-motivated extremists in the trade unions sought a direct confrontation with a Conservative government, "they will be resisted firmly and decisively" (Howe *et al.* 1977: 14, 16). Thatcher insisted that this policy document was only published on the firm basis that it was *not* to be presented as an official shadow cabinet statement (Shepherd 1991: 180; TF 1977a).

Meanwhile, on the issue of pay determination, rather than commit to continued incomes policies, *The Right Approach to the Economy* pledged "a policy for earnings" whereby a "return to realistic collective bargaining" would be pursued in tandem with "some kind of forum ... where the major participants in the economy can sit down calmly together to consider the implications" of pay increases in the context of broader economic conditions and governmental commitments to controlling the money supply and public expenditure in order to reduce inflation (Howe *et al.* 1977: 12).

Thatcher's path to 10 Downing Street

Two specific factors eventually paved the way for the Conservative Party's victory in the May 1979 general election, namely the decision by the Labour prime minister, James Callaghan, *not* to call a general election in autumn 1978, and the "winter of discontent", which refers to a series of strikes, mostly by local government and public sector workers, during January and February 1979. Although seemingly distinct, and a few months apart, the two were interlinked, as we will briefly explain, and together were instrumental in enabling Thatcher to become prime minister.

The Labour government had been re-elected in October 1974 with a mere three seat parliamentary majority, and this soon disappeared due to by-election defeats, a few MPs defecting to other parties (such as Reg Prentice, who defected to the Conservatives, claiming that Labour was being infiltrated by Marxists), and the deaths of a couple of Labour MPs. Vulnerable to defeat on any key division (parliamentary vote), Labour entered into a pact with the Liberal Party, whereby the Liberals' 14 MPs would support Labour in votes on key issues, in return for being consulted on a range of policies, and would also be permitted to propose a few policies of their own (Dorey 2011; Kirkup 2015). The Lib–Lab pact, as it was known, operated from March 1977 to July 1978, whereupon it was terminated. This immediately raised expectations that the ailing minority Labour government would call a general election, probably in the autumn, in the hope of securing a proper parliamentary majority. Certainly, several of the Conservative shadow cabinet's meetings during the spring and summer of 1978 were understandably focused on discussing the party's manifesto for the anticipated 1978 election, and thus ensuring that it was fully prepared (see, e.g., TF 1978b, 1978c, 1978d, 1978e, 1978f).

However, after poring over both public and private polling data during August 1978, and eliciting the views of his cabinet colleagues (who were themselves divided over whether to call the election in the autumn, or wait until 1979 in the hope that economic and political conditions would have improved), Callaghan decided against calling a general election, opting instead to wait until spring 1979 (on Callaghan's anguished deliberations, and the factors influencing his decision, see Dorey 2016a). Three factors informed this decision. First, although a couple of opinion polls about voting intentions did report a narrow Labour lead, the overwhelming majority of them suggested that either the Conservatives would narrowly win, or there would be another hung parliament in which the largest party would be dependent on the support of the minor parties (see Pack n.d.). Not surprisingly, the ultra-cautious Callaghan judged an autumn 1978 general election to be far too risky for Labour. Second, Callaghan envisaged that the economic situation would have improved by the spring of 1979, and that an increasing feel-good factor among voters would be reinforced by a benevolent Budget, perhaps coupled with warmer days and lighter evenings.

Crucially, and fatally as it turned out, the third factor influencing Callaghan's decision *not* to call an autumn 1978 general election was his expectation that the trade unions would tolerate a fourth successive year of wage restraint, via a 5 per cent pay policy for the next year, in order to maximize Labour's chances of defeating the Conservatives in a 1979 general election. The rationale was that if an election "was still pending, Callaghan had something to hold over them … If they started striking, that could mean we lost, and they got Margaret Thatcher. So they had an incentive to play ball" (Lipsey 2012: 126). It proved to be catastrophic miscalculation, and according to one of Callaghan's ministerial colleagues, Shirley Williams, derived from "a tragic over-estimation of his own influence with the trade unions leaders, and of their influence over their members" (Williams 2010: 248).

Certainly, Callaghan seemed to have misjudged the extent to which he could secure continued trade union acquiescence by portraying Margaret Thatcher as a spectre who the unions should fear, because in the context of Labour's continued reliance on wage restraint to conquer inflation, a growing number of trade unionists were becoming rather receptive to the Conservatives' advocacy of a return to free collective bargaining between workers and their employers. Many of the lowest-paid viewed continued incomes policies as perpetuating their poverty, while sections of the skilled working class (the C2s, or what Lenin referred to unflatteringly as a labour aristocracy) had grown to resent the erosion of the differentials they had traditionally enjoyed over less-skilled workers, and were thus increasingly attracted to the Thatcherite promise that pay would be more directly linked to skills and talent. Indeed, the largest swing to the Conservatives in May 1979 was among the skilled working class.

The winter of discontent entailed a series of strikes by various local government and public sector workers at the start of 1979, and because of the workers involved and the services affected, the disruption caused was often both highly visual in terms of media reportage, and sometimes distressing to affected members of the public. With regard to the former, for example, industrial action by local council refuse collectors led to household and commercial rubbish, albeit often in flimsy bin-bags, being piled in the street, and posing a health risk as they attracted rats, and/or could easily be torn open by other animals, causing rotting food to be strewn across pavements. In terms of personal distress, strikes by gravediggers reportedly resulted in funerals being postponed, adding to the grief of mourning family members.

We use the word "reportedly" in the previous sentence because some writers have argued that the winter of discontent became part of a right-wing or Thatcherite anti-union narrative or discourse – aided and abetted by pro-Conservative newspapers – which depicted individual or local events and hardships as endemic; far more widespread, disruptive, and distressing to many more people, than was really the case (Hay 1996; Lopez 2014). This narrative and discourse also invoked the populist device of constructing binary opposites and polarities; "them" and "us" – "them" being over-mighty or selfish trade unions and their militant leaders holding the country to ransom, and "us" being the innocent and powerless members of the public whose rubbish was not being collected, and in the case of the recently bereaved, were being denied the right to bury their dead relatives or spouse due to graves not being dug. In its most apocalyptic or sensational form, the narrative depicted the British nation and its people as being under siege from the unions, and also from subversives or extremists who hoped that industrial action would precipitate the overthrow of capitalism.

Meanwhile, some senior ministers in the Labour government subsequently conceded that they had to bear some responsibility for the winter of discontent because of their insistence on persevering with an unrealistic pay limit following three years of increasingly unpopular incomes policies and wage restraint. As the then chancellor, Denis Healey, himself later reflected, although the "cowardice and irresponsibility of some union leaders at this time [winter 1978–79] guaranteed her [Margaret Thatcher's] election", and "left them with no grounds for complaining about her subsequent actions against them", it was also the case that "we in the cabinet should have realized that our five per cent pay norm would be provocative as well as unattainable". With hindsight, he acknowledged that: "If we had been content with a formula like 'single figures', we would have had lower settlements, have avoided the winter of discontent, and probably have won the [May 1979] election too" (Healey 1990: 462–3).

This last point is highly significant, because it indicates that prior to the winter of discontent, Thatcher's victory in the 1979 general election was not inevitable, in spite of the small lead that the Conservative Party enjoyed in sundry opinion polls during the autumn of 1978, and which had been instrumental in Callaghan's fateful decision to defer calling a general election. Had the winter of discontent not occurred, and the economic situation had continued slowly improving, it is quite likely that the Labour government would have been re-elected. For example, in December 1978, a Gallup poll reported a 5 percentage point Conservative lead over Labour (48 to 43), but by mid-February, this had been transformed into a 20 point Conservative lead (53 to 33) (see Pack n.d.).

As William Whitelaw reflected, many voters had hitherto been apprehensive about voting for Margaret Thatcher's Conservative Party, partly due to fear that the Conservatives would provoke industrial conflict by supposedly bashing the unions. However, he claimed that the bitter experience of the winter of discontent fatally undermined Labour's claim, in the 1974 general elections, that it was the only party which could work harmoniously with the trade unions. Instead, many voters now wanted the trade unions reformed (curbed), while many union members themselves welcomed the promised rejection of incomes policies in favour of a return to free collective bargaining: "It needed further hard experience, culminating in the Winter of Discontent ... before the British people were ready to give continuous backing to a government for trade union reform" (Whitelaw 1989: 185–6; see also Clarke 2016: 103).

2

The development of Thatcherism: intellectual origins and ideological framework

As we have seen, Thatcher was not yet a Thatcherite when elected as Conservative leader in February 1975, and even by 1979, some of her political ideas were still developing, although her ideological inclination was clearly evident. Thatcherism developed incrementally, in a step-by-step manner, although her strides became longer and quicker as her confidence grew, particularly when she also realized how ineffective her political opponents were, both inside the Conservative Party, and beyond. Thatcherism derived from an eclectic array of individual, institutional and intellectual sources, as well as being facilitated, and in some respects lent credence or credibility, by circumstances and events.

Her disillusionment with the 1970–74 Heath government (in which she had been education secretary) naturally prompted her reconsideration of British Conservatism, and in undertaking this critical reflection, she was strongly influenced and encouraged by the similarly disillusioned Keith Joseph, who introduced her to the key intellectual sources of neoliberalism: Milton Freidman, Friedrich Hayek and Adam Smith. Thatcher already instinctively or intuitively agreed with many of their ideas, but under Joseph's tutelage, and through reading the texts of these neoliberal economists and political theorists, her beliefs became more systematic and substantive.

These ideas were also being proselytized in the 1970s by free-market think tanks such as the Adam Smith Institute, established in 1977 (Pirie 2012), and the Institute of Economic Affairs, the latter formed in 1955, but acquiring much greater prominence and credence in the context of the serious economic problems facing Britain in the 1970s (Seldon 1981; Desai 1994). Of course, Thatcher, Joseph and Sherman also formed, in 1974, their own think tank, the Centre for Policy Studies, which promoted what subsequently became Thatcherism. These three think tanks are still active today.

The quest for a new or true Conservatism

It was after Edward Heath's Conservative government had lost the February 1974 general election (followed by another Conservative defeat in that year's October general election) that Keith Joseph had his Damascene conversion to what he now considered to be true Conservatism: "it was only in April 1974 that I was converted to Conservatism. I had thought that I was a Conservative, but I now see that I was not really one at all" (Joseph 1975: 4). This realization was buttressed by his convivial meetings with a former communist, Alfred Sherman, who, having visited Yugoslavia (part of the former Soviet Union's geopolitical bloc) in the late 1940s, became a born-again convert to free-market economics and passionate advocate of individual liberty against the power of the state (Beckett 2009: 280).

The two men formed a close intellectual and ideological bond during 1974, as Sherman extolled the virtues of economic freedom and private enterprise, and helped Joseph to transform his instinctive disillusionment with postwar Conservatism in general, and the Heath government in particular, into a more cogent critique of postwar British political economy. Joseph and Sherman were occasionally joined by another enthusiastic advocate of free-market economics, Alan Walters, and it was apparently the latter who ultimately convinced Joseph that controlling the money supply was the key to curbing inflation, rather than the erstwhile pursuit of incomes policies (Cockett 1995: 233; Beckett 2009: 281).

Through Joseph, Thatcher also became acquainted with Sherman, who similarly proselytized the case for a new direction for the Conservative Party by "plotting out a new kind of free-market Conservatism", a task he pursued, Thatcher recalled, with "a convert's zeal" (Thatcher 1995: 251). Thatcher proved highly receptive to Sherman's analysis of how, why and where post-1945 Britain and the Conservative Party had apparently pursued the wrong policies derived from erroneous assumptions. It was also through Joseph that Thatcher was acquainted with Norman Strauss and John Hoskyns, both of whom also became integral to the development of Thatcherism in general, and for developing a strategy for tackling the trade unions in particular, the latter being judged a prerequisite of achieving many other key policy objectives (Sherman Papers 1976).

The close personal and political bond between Joseph and Sherman yielded the 1974 formation of the Centre for Policy Studies (CPS), a combative think tank which simultaneously promoted market economics in the name of freedom, but greater individual responsibility to restore social discipline and what became known as family values. In establishing the CPS, Joseph and Sherman appointed Thatcher as vice-chair of the think tank, which, she recalled: "acted as a focus for a large group of free-market thinkers ... who sought to change the climate of opinion and achieve wider understanding of the role of the market and the shortcomings of statism ... to expose the follies and self-defeating consequences of government intervention" (Thatcher 1995: 250–51).

Thatcher's own intellectual and ideological conversion was relatively straightforward, because her family background and upbringing in the Lincolnshire town of Grantham, where her father was owner and proprietor of a corner-shop, had inculcated moral values which lauded hard work, frugality, self-reliance, sobriety and thrift – what the Conservative philosopher Shirley Letwin (1992: 33) termed "vigorous virtues". Crucially, Thatcher instinctively believed that these corner-shop and small-town principles could and should be applied to the nation's economy and society's moral framework.

Thatcher shared Joseph's deep disappointment with the dirigiste policies subsequently adopted by the Heath government after it had been elected on a seemingly free-market, limited state, manifesto in June 1970. Thatcher and Joseph were certainly not alone in their despondency; another senior Conservative, Jock Bruce-Gardyne (1974), ruefully enquired "whatever happened to the quiet revolution?" that the Conservative leadership had seemingly promised in the 1970 general election. Enoch Powell had also been scathing, particularly in sundry parliamentary speeches, about the Heath government's reversion to dirigisme and incomes policies prior to defecting to the Ulster Unionists.

Sherman immediately recognized how receptive Thatcher was, because the "first eighteen years of her life in Puritan England shaped her for ever" and having "brought Grantham with her ... much of Grantham was embodied within her, waiting to emerge" (Sherman 2005: 86; see also Biddiss 1987: 2; Young & Sloman 1986: 20–21). As one non-Thatcherite minister in the 1980s recalls, for many Conservative MPs, "the economics that she had learned from her father, Alderman

Roberts, behind the grocer's counter, were part of their DNA. Keynes was associated with fiscal irresponsibility, or, worse, socialist depravity" (Patten 2018: 142). A more sympathetic minister in the Thatcher governments Kenneth Baker, recalled that: "To understand Margaret, you have to go back to Grantham. She lived in a very humble way. There are not many grocers' daughters who get to Somerville College Oxford to study chemistry", a feat which "required incredible drive and determination" (quoted in BBC2 2019a).

As one of her most eminent academic biographers explained: "A small shop … displays the working of the market in its purest form. Just as farm children gain early familiarity with reproduction, the child of a shopkeeper cannot grow up ignorant of the facts of economic life" (Campbell 2000: 10). Meanwhile, one of Thatcher's private secretaries, Caroline Slocock, reflected that initially, "one of her strengths was that she came from an ordinary background, and she brought that authenticity" to the premiership (BBC 2019b).

Although Sherman was immediately impressed by Thatcher's instinctive views and values, and her receptiveness to new ideas which challenged post-1945 economic orthodoxy, he also underestimated her, because he doubted whether she had ever read Hayek, whereas she had actually been reading Hayek's [1944] *The Road to Serfdom* sporadically since the late 1940s. However, she confessed that it was not until the mid-1970s that she "fully grasped the implications of Hayek's little masterpiece". Indeed, Thatcher recalled that during the mid-1970s, "Hayek's works were right at the top of the reading list given me by Keith Joseph", whereupon "I really came to grips with the ideas he [Hayek] put forward" and learned to "consider his arguments from the point of view of the kind of state Conservatives find congenial – a limited government under a rule of law" (Thatcher 1995: 50).

On one occasion, John Ranelagh recalls that when she was visiting the Conservative Research Department a few months after being elected party leader, an official began extolling the virtues of the "middle way" between left and right as the path for Conservatives to follow, whereupon Thatcher retrieved a copy of Hayek's *The Constitution of Liberty* from her briefcase, ostentatiously held it aloft and declared that: "This is what we believe", before slamming it down on the table (quoted in Cockett 1995: 174). As Sherman recalled, by the mid-1970s, rather than directly prompting Thatcher's increasing conversion to neoliberalism, her re-reading of Hayek (and Milton Friedman) "provided reinforcement for principles she already held instinctively" (Sherman 2005: 25; see also Biddiss 1987: 6; Joseph quoted in Young & Sloman 1986: 60). Or as Harrison (1994: 217) noted: "Political philosophy (Hayek) and monetarist theory (Friedman) chimed in with, articulated and provided a framework of action for sentiments that arose from personal instincts and practical situations. For Thatcher, formal theories coincided with inclinations long present, supplementing ... [and] ... providing intellectual backing for a course already decided upon".

Looking back to this period, Thatcher (1995: 254) readily acknowledged that: "From Keith and Alfred, I learned a great deal. I renewed my reading of the seminal works of liberal economics and conservative thought". Or as she reminisced to one of her special advisers in the Number 10 Policy Unit: "Dear Keith, such a wonderful source of ideas. He taught me such a lot" (Mount 2008: 286).

It was Sherman who also introduced Thatcher to John Hoskyns, a politically disillusioned businessman, and who subsequently became a senior special adviser in the Number 10 Policy Unit during her early premiership. However, Hoskyns initially judged Thatcher to be "very disappointing ... She is a limited, pedantic bore, with no lateral grasp, very little humour ... God help the Tories" (TF 1976a), although he was subsequently less harsh about this meeting in his memoir/diaries (Hoskyns 2000: 24, diary entry for 25 September 1976). The initial negative impression was fully reciprocated, although Thatcher soon "came to appreciate the depth and quality of John Hoskyns' analysis" (Thatcher 1995: 420).

During the mid-1970s, Thatcher also "regularly attended lunches at the Institute of Economic Affairs, where Ralph Harris, Arthur Seldon, Alan Walters, and others ... were busy marking out a new non-socialist economic and social path for Britain" (Thatcher 1995: 254). As one commentator noted, looking back to this era, she "became a fixed point within a kaleidoscope of informal groupings – university teachers ... activists within the Centre for Policy Studies, or weekly lunchers at the Institute of Economic Affairs" (Harrison 1994: 209; see also Jackson 2012; King 1985: 126–7).

The ideas that Thatcher imbibed from people like "Alan Walters, Keith Joseph and Alfred Sherman – and behind them, Enoch Powell and the thinkers in Vienna [Hayek], Chicago [Friedman], and at the

Institute of Economic Affairs – were instrumental" in imbuing her instinctive economic views and Grantham corner-shop experiences with intellectual rigour and validation (Ranelagh 1992: 212). Thatcher herself recalled that she had "always been an instinctive Conservative, but I failed to develop these instincts either into a coherent framework of ideas or into a set of practical policies for government" (Thatcher 1993: 14). She subsequently acknowledged that, just as Keith Joseph could not "have achieved what he did without the Centre for Policy Studies and Alfred Sherman", she "could not have become Leader of the opposition or achieved what I did as prime minister, without Keith" (Thatcher 1993: 251; see also Ranelagh 1992: 214).

A major reason why Thatcher readily accepted the ideas and analyses of these key individuals and think tanks – quite apart from the fact that they reflected and reinforced her own instincts and developing intellectual outlook – was the view, shared by all of them, that the Conservative Research Department (CRD) was a bastion of Heathite wetness, and thus wholly unreliable as a source of new and radical ideas; indeed, there was a suspicion that the CRD would actively seek to undermine the change of political direction that Thatcher and her allies were clearly developing, especially as it was headed by the decidedly non-Thatcherite Chris Patten (Cowling 1990: xxv; Hoskyns 2000: 56; Sherman 2005: 82; Thatcher 1995: 292; TF 1978g).

A notable aspect of Thatcher's Conservative leadership and subsequent premiership was her readiness, in speeches, to cite some of the intellectuals and sources which underpinned her ideology. For example, in a parliamentary debate on the economic situation in mid-1970s Britain, Thatcher cited the academics Robert Bacon and Walter Eltis to support her claim that "we can no longer go on tinkering with the economy but we have to look at the real structural changes which are needed" (Hansard 1976, Vol. 917, col. 149), while in 1981, during a weekly Prime Minister's Questions, Thatcher declared that "I am a great admirer of Professor Hayek. Some of his books are absolutely supreme – *The Constitution of Liberty* and the three volumes on *Law, Legislation and Liberty* – and would be well read by almost every hon. Member [of parliament]" (Hansard 1981, Vol. 1000: col. 756).

Thatcher also used a (1977) Iain Macleod Memorial Lecture to extol the free-market ideas of Adam Smith (TF 1977a), and in a 1984 speech at the Carlton Club, praised Adam Smith as the "greatest" of political economists, due to his understanding of how a market economy both devolves and disperses power, and maximizes consumer choice and freedom (TF 1984a).

Yet while Thatcher readily cited her intellectual progenitors, she also frequently depicted her ideas and policies as mere "common sense", and thereby imbued them with a broader popular – and populist – appeal. Just a few weeks after being elected as party leader, Thatcher explained to Conservative Central Office that: "This is our doctrine. The doctrine of common sense in a free society" (TF 1975c). Two years later, she asserted that "the Conservative Party is the party of common sense" (TF 1977b), a claim that she repeated the following year, when she pledged that a Conservative government would "tackle each problem as it arises with practical common sense" (TF 1978a; see also TF 1978h). The pledges subsequently enshrined in the Conservatives' 1979 manifesto were deemed, according to Thatcher's foreword, to be based "not on dogma, but on reason, on common sense" (Conservative Party 1979: 5).

Thatcher continued to invoke common sense to explain and legitimize her government's policies throughout her premiership, doing so regularly in parliamentary and public speeches, and via media interviews. To give just one more example, at a 1985 Prime Minister's Questions, she reiterated that "it is common sense that one must have policies which pursue the creation of wealth, before that wealth can be distributed" (Hansard 1985, Vol. 76, cols 210–11). Of course, by invoking common sense to justify her governments' policies, Thatcher was simultaneously seeking to obfuscate their ideological content and objectives, while also implying that her political opponents lacked common sense.

Rejecting post-1945 political economy, state intervention and egalitarianism

The Thatcherite advocacy of the free market and private enterprise, including the veneration of profit and maximization of shareholder value as the *sin qua non* of economic activity, naturally entailed a rejection of the principles and policies on which much postwar economic and industrial policy had been based, and which successive Conservatives had broadly subscribed to in accordance with such values as continuity, moderation, pragmatism and stability, these reflecting and reinforcing the pre-Thatcher Conservative Party's emphatic eschewal of ideology and teleological blueprints for radical socio-economic reconstruction. However, Thatcher and Joseph were adamant that this non-ideological stance had unwittingly enabled the left to seize the initiative, set the political agenda, and determine the policy direction travelled by post-war Britain, including its Conservative governments. For nascent Thatcherites, therefore, it was vital for the Conservative Party to become much more proactive and combative, and thereupon change course by directly challenging the alleged ideological dominance of the left, and its apparent colonization of key civic and political institutions.

Fundamental to Thatcherism was hostility to the state's postwar role in economic management, and the associated orthodoxy of Keynesianism to boost demand through governmental spending (funded by high taxation, discussed below), and to promote full employment. This hostility was intrinsic to neoliberalism, but in the 1970s, was seemingly buttressed by empirical developments and practical problems which were afflicting the British economy, and, in turn, raising concerns about whether Britain was becoming ungovernable. The interventionist state was deemed to be crowding out the wealth-creating private sector, while the size and cost of the public sector and nationalized industries were further weakening the British economy, leaving it with "too few producers", the latter deemed to be the ultimate wealth-creators (Bacon & Eltis 1976). Keith Joseph strongly agreed with this perspective, asserting that since 1945: "The private sector, the productive sector, has been weighed down by the burden of taxation, by the burden of subsidies to nationalized industries. The public sector has been draining away the wealth created by the private sector" (Joseph 1975: 7).

Thatcherism argued that most of the economic and social problems which the postwar state had increasingly intervened to eradicate were ultimately caused or exacerbated by the state itself. Joseph and Thatcher insisted that much of the economic history of postwar Britain was not a record of repeated free market failure, but of relentless intervention by the state which prevented the free market from thriving in the first place. In other words, the state frequently intervened to tackle problems which had ultimately been caused or compounded by its previous intervention, but which were then blamed on deficiencies in the market and the private sector. Thatcherites therefore decreed that state intervention was cumulative and self-reinforcing, dragging Britain along what Hayek had identified as the "the road to serfdom" (Hayek 1944).

Thatcher informed the West Midlands Conservatives in the autumn of 1975 that: "The Socialists claim that [state intervention] is necessary because capitalism has failed the nation. But what we face today is not a crisis of capitalism, but of socialism" (TF 1975d). This echoed a point trenchantly articulated by Enoch Powell a decade earlier, when he had insisted that: "The politician's duty ... is not to rush around trying to supplant the profit motive. Either by coaxing others or by trying to do the job himself ... It is to find out ... what it is that is stopping the profit motive from working ... Quite often the blockage will turn out to be some interference or series of interferences for which he or his predecessors are responsible" (quoted in Wood 1965: 82).

In condemning state intervention, the emerging Thatcherite critique of postwar British political economy pointed to the inherent tendency towards monopolies which ensued when governments assumed responsibility for running major industries via nationalization, and providing public services such as education and health care. This further crowded-out the private sector, and left many industries and most public services almost entirely devoid of the competition or consumer sovereignty, which supposedly spurred private sector companies to innovate and constantly strive to improve their products or service, or reduce their prices, to attract and then retain more customers than their rivals. Without such competition, Thatcherites argued, state-owned industries and the public sector had no incentive to improve their quality or otherwise offer a better service, because their customers were, in effect, a captive clientele.

Furthermore, whereas in the private sector a loss of customers, due to poor service or high prices, led ultimately to lower profits and job losses, this market discipline was absent from those industries and services owned or provided by the state, because they were funded by tax revenues, which governments themselves largely determined; if a nationalized industry or public service faced financial difficulties, Thatcherites complained, then ministers would invariably increase borrowing or taxation to fund the shortfall. There was no apparent compunction for the state to improve cost-effectiveness, efficiency, or financial rectitude in nationalized industries and the public sector.

Rejection of high income taxes

According to Thatcherites, the sheer scale and combined cost of state-owned industries, the public sector, and the welfare state, were the main reason why direct taxes were deemed to be too high in the 1970s, and seemed to be on an inexorably upward trajectory, even while governments disingenuously depicted public services as being free. Yet Thatcherism fundamentally rejected high taxation of incomes and profits, both in principle, and because of the practical consequences. As a matter of principle, the neoliberal aspect of Thatcherism deemed it morally and politically wrong that the state should take too much of people's earnings or other sources of income, and then decide how this money should be spent, rather than permitting individuals to retain more of what they earned or legitimately acquired, and thereupon make their own choices and decisions about how to spend their income. In effect, taxation was a necessary evil which should be minimized, with governments, ideally, only taxing people and profits in order to fund activities and services which could not be provided individually or profitably by the private sector, such as indivisible public goods like policing to maintain internal order via the rule of law, and defence to ensure security from military attack by external enemies.

Beyond this, Thatcherism held that as far as practicably possible, many services provided by the state could, and should, be purchased and provided privately, most notably education, health care, housing, pensions and transport. Furthermore, if private provision of such services could be increased, then the reduced role of the state would mean that it required less income from taxation, and, in turn, if people were paying less tax, then their increased net pay and disposable income would enable many more of them to go private. Ideologically, the two ostensibly distinct policy objectives of cutting direct taxation and extending the free market, via the private provision of formerly public services, became interlinked and mutually reinforcing.

However, Thatcherism advanced a more practical reason for promoting income tax cuts, namely that the high rates of taxation in the latter half of the 1970s, when the top rate was 83 per cent and the basic rate was 33 per cent, were not only morally indefensible, but counterproductive, because of the extent to which this deterred entrepreneurship and hard work. The Thatcherite argument here was that the rich and businesspeople were deterred from investing and creating wealth, because their profits and/or salaries were taxed so heavily that the effort, energy and risks were not worthwhile. Yet if entrepreneurs and the rich were penalized through high taxation, then they would cease to invest or spend as much, which would prevent the trickle down of wealth from which the rest of society apparently benefited. Here, we can also discern Adam Smith's claim that the pursuit of self-interest and personal enrichment, instead of being selfish, actually benefits society by satisfying the material needs of the other citizens: "It is not from the benevolence of the butcher, the brewer, or the baker that we expect our dinner, but from their regard to their own interest" (Smith 1986: 119).

At the same time, however, Thatcherism argued that high rates of income tax – in tandem with allegedly generous social security benefits – were a deterrent to the poor or low-paid, because after income tax and national insurance had been deducted from their wages, some ordinary workers were left with little more than they would receive in welfare payments if they were unemployed. As such, supposedly excessive taxation contributed to the "why work?" syndrome, whereby some potential workers allegedly decided that they might as well as remain unemployed and live off social security benefits, because work "did not pay". This, in turn created resentment among those who did undertake relatively low-paid jobs, due to the perception – encouraged by Conservatives and much of the press (even today, as an integral aspect of their divide and rule strategy) – that a major reason why a third of their weekly wage was being taxed was the cost of funding so-called welfare scroungers. Consequently, the rich and working poor alike were courted with the promise of significant income tax cuts, and the accompanying pledge that their hard work would henceforth make them much better-off financially, especially in the context of a parallel pledge to clampdown on the so-called dependency culture fostered by the welfare state.

A new critique of the cause of inflation

Prior to the mid-1970s, it had been widely accepted that the prime cause of inflation was high wage increases, whereupon companies increased their prices to cover their higher labour costs. The result of this supposedly cost-push inflation was that a vicious circle was activated, whereby wage claims by trade unions led employers to raise prices, which then led to even higher pay claims by the union leaders to offset the increased cost of living. It was in response to this scenario that successive governments had resorted to incomes policies, of various stringency and complexity, which entailed a specified pay limit being set each year, the precise figure either being announced and imposed unilaterally by ministers, or agreed via trilateral negotiations between trade union leaders (via the TUC's General Council), major employers (via the Confederation of Industry – CBI) and government ministers. Yet the longer or more stringently that incomes policies were imposed, the more resentment they aroused among trade unionists, to the extent that they eventually broke down, until another surge of inflation prompted a new incomes policy, and the cycle repeated itself (for the chequered history of incomes policies in Britain, see Dorey 2001).

Although some senior figures in Thatcher's Conservative Party continued to view incomes policies as an essential means of conquering inflation, Thatcher and her steadily expanding coterie of ideological converts were increasingly rejecting them. The economic neoliberalism which informed and underpinned Thatcherism rejected the premise that inflation was caused by wage increases fuelling higher prices, and instead argued that it was ultimately a consequence of excessive increases in the money supply, fuelled by governments spending too much, often by printing more money than the economy could absorb in the context of low growth and productivity. In effect, with too much money chasing too few goods and products, prices increased. This seemingly new perspective had been enunciated by the ultra-neoliberal Enoch Powell back in the latter half of the 1960s, when he had insisted that inflation was "politician-made", rather than caused directly by the trade unions. As such, he had deemed incomes policies to reflect a fundamental misunderstanding or ignorance about the underlying cause of inflation (Powell 1969: chs 8–9; Wood 1965: ch. 11).

By the mid-1970s, Powell's critique, echoed by the ideas and theories of economists like Milton Friedman (1962: ch. 3; Friedman & Friedman 1980: ch. 9), was becoming more widely accepted among some senior Conservatives, especially Thatcher and Joseph. For example, Thatcher (1995: 141) subsequently conceded that: "Enoch was right. He had made the … intellectual leaps in economic policy which Keith Joseph and I would only make some years later … he had grasped that it was not the unions which cause inflation by pushing up wages, but rather the government which did so by increasing the supply of money in the economy. Consequently, incomes policies … were a supreme irrelevance to anti-inflation policy".

Joseph fully agreed, reiterating that: "When the money supply grows too quickly, inflation results … to create too much money … is to court the danger of inflation". This rendered incomes policy ineffective as the means of curbing inflation, because curbing the money supply was what was essential; relying on incomes policy "as a way to abate inflation caused by excessive money supply is like trying to stop water coming out of a leaky hose without turning off the tap" (Joseph 1975: 20–21; see also Biffen 1977; Ridley 1976).

Yet if trade unions were not the prime cause of inflation, that did not mean that neoliberals condoned supposedly excessive pay rises. On the contrary, it was argued that while such wage increases were not inflationary *per se*, they would cause job losses and higher unemployment once politicians ceased to spend and print more money to sustain or boost consumer demand. If trade unions continued pursuing pay rises which were higher than what their company or employer could afford in the context of its profitability – unless there was a corresponding increase in productivity – then the consequence would be that some workers would, in effect, price themselves out of work, and unemployment would increase.

For Thatcherites, this would serve to teach trade unions and workers a vital lesson, namely that wages and salaries were dependent on market criteria, and that the only realistic means of increasing incomes was to work harder, increase productivity, and thereby boost profitability. This, it was assumed, would eventually have a far more salutary and educative effect on trade unionists than any incomes policy or ministerial speeches exhorting pay restraint. As Nicholas Ridley explained, "people must be made to suffer the consequences of their actions, or inaction, once more" (Ridley 1974; see also Ridley 1976: 12; Price 1977). Or as Keith Joseph bluntly explained, trade unions should be "free to price their people out of jobs, or bankrupt their employers, if their members really wished them to" (quoted in *The Times*, 1 April 1976). Here, as in many other spheres, Thatcherites were adamant that individuals should take responsibility for their own actions, and accept the consequences.

Eschewing egalitarianism

A further feature of the Thatcherite critique of post-1945 British politics and policies was the emphatic rejection of egalitarianism, which had entailed the pursuit of greater equality primarily via wealth redistribution, high taxation of the rich and a comprehensive welfare state, and thus narrowing the gap between rich and poor. Although this policy objective had been naturally embraced by the Labour Party, it had also been partly accepted, at least in practice, by One Nation Conservatives, both as a manifestation of the noblesse oblige which characterized many of them, entailing an acceptance that the rich had a duty of care towards the poor, and partly due to electoral politics, whereby it was assumed *a priori* that a dual commitment to tackling poverty and promoting a fairer society would reap dividends in general elections. The One Nation Conservatives continued to reject equality philosophically, both on the grounds that inequality was both intrinsic to human nature, and necessary to provide incentives and rewards for hard work and leadership roles, but they also acknowledged that too much inequality – albeit never defining what constituted too much – was likely to undermine the legitimacy of capitalism and parliamentary democracy, and might render the working class vulnerable to the seductive siren call of Marxism or other radical ideologies (Dorey 2010a: ch. 2; see also Gilmour 1992: 276–9).

This stance was firmly rejected by Thatcherites, who believed that egalitarianism had become an obsession in post-1945 Britain, and was also further evidence of the alleged dominance of pro-equality left-wing ideas among opinion-formers, political elites and social scientists. In 1975, future chancellor, Nigel Lawson complained that the pursuit of equality had become "the great bug bear of our time", while the Conservative philosopher, Roger Scruton, identified egalitarianism as the "most important" of the "contagions" which had afflicted Britain's body politic since 1945 (TF 1975e; Scruton 1984: 59).

Thatcherites attributed the alleged postwar obsession with equality to two factors, one of which was the advocacy of social justice, and the other was simply the promotion of the politics of envy, both of which were supposedly perpetrated by the left. With regard to the former, it was variously noted that the left often invoked the notion of social justice – in tandem with calls for fairness – when condemning "excessive" inequality of earnings and incomes. Yet the notion of social justice was emphatically rejected by Hayek, when he insisted that the allocation of earnings, incomes and wealth through market mechanisms "can be neither just nor unjust, because the results are not intended or foreseen, and depend on a multitude of circumstances not known in their totality to anybody" (Hayek 1976: 70). Or as he later expressed it, because incomes, in a free society, are determined via the natural mechanisms of the free market, it is "meaningless to call this spontaneous order unjust … It is simply not capable of bearing such an attribute. Only human actions can be just or unjust", and as such, he considered "social" (as in "social" justice) to be a "weasel word" used disingenuously by those who wanted to impose equality (Hayek 1988: 52). In similar vein, Robert Moss, then leader of the (vehemently anti-socialist) Freedom Association, argued that: "The idea that the role of government is to impose social justice has contributed to the derangement of the state in modern Britain" (Moss 1978: 142–3).

Keith Joseph fully shared Hayek's dismissive view of social justice and the underlying motive attributed to its advocates. In 1975, Joseph had given a speech at the London School of Economics on the theme of "the tyranny hidden in the pursuit of equality", in which he insisted that there is "no way of assessing such intangibles as merit or effort without giving someone arbitrary and discretionary powers to decide who is worth how much", which begged the question "Who is to judge?" (quoted in Halcrow 1989: 105; see also Joseph & Sumption 1979).

The second aspect of the Thatcherite counterattack against the postwar pursuit of egalitarianism was to impugn the motives of those advocating (greater) equality, and thereby discredit them; a classic ad hominem tactic beloved of the right; play the (wo)man, not the ball. In this context, it was commonly alleged that egalitarians were usually motivated primarily by the politics of envy. According to Joseph, for example, it was frequently the case that "the attitudes and motives that nourish egalitarian politics" are "pursuit of power, envy of those who are different, passion for domination", these "adding up to a hatred of diversity. Of such motives are tyrants made" (Joseph 1976: 79; see also Joseph & Sumption 1979; Brittan 1983: 71–2). Similarly, in a speech in New York during her first year as Conservative leader, Thatcher alleged that advocates of equality were often motivated by "envy … clearly at work in the case of the egalitarian who resents the gap between himself and those who are better off" (TF 1975f). The Conservative Party's 1979 election manifesto repeated the allegation, accusing the 1974–79 Labour government of "practising the politics of envy", and claiming that in so doing, "they have set one group against another" (Conservative Party 1979: 6).

Thatcherites also argued that Britain's increasingly poor industrial performance since 1945 was partly due to the extent to which entrepreneurial wealth creators had been deterred or driven overseas by the pursuit of equality, and associated policies, such as high rates of income tax and wealth redistribution. Would-be employers and wealth-creating business leaders had apparently decided not to invest in Britain because of the extent to which any fortune they amassed would be appropriated by the state. As Thatcher explained, Britain in the 1970s was suffering from "thirty years of concentrating on [wealth] distribution … at the price of not putting enough into the growth of the economy and creating wealth", a fatal policy priority which had also entailed "transferring far too much from the private sector into the public sector" (TF 1975f).

The logical Thatcherite corollary, therefore, was that the policies associated with egalitarianism and wealth redistribution needed to be abandoned, whereupon entrepreneurs and business leaders would be entitled to keep much more of what they earned in return for successfully generating more economic growth, investment and profits. This, in turn, would benefit millions of ordinary British people via more employment opportunities and the much-vaunted trickle down of wealth; indeed, this would supposedly benefit them much more directly and tangibly than the policies associated with egalitarianism. Or as Joseph and Jonathan Sumption (1976: 22) argued, "you cannot make the poor richer by making the rich poorer. You can only make the poor richer by making everyone richer, including the rich".

In all these spheres, the discourse was about rolling back the state, setting people free, and maximizing individual liberty, in order to promote entrepreneurship and wealth creation, encourage small businesses, and increase opportunities for people to pursue their legitimate economic interests. However, as we note in the next chapter, the promotion of a free-market economy also necessitated a strong or interventionist state to challenge institutions which were deemed an impediment to the operation of the free market, such as trade unions. In some respects, therefore, the state was not so much rolled back as restructured (Gamble 1988: 231–6).

The advocacy of social discipline and traditional morality

While strongly denouncing the scale and scope of state intervention in economic and industrial affairs since 1945, Thatcherism equally condemned the state's alleged failure to defend and maintain moral values and social discipline. A growing number of Conservative politicians, and ideologically-aligned academics or journalists, complained that in postwar Britain, the state had eviscerated individual liberty in economic affairs through its determination to exercise ever greater control over the market, while allowing too much freedom in the social realm, especially since the 1960s, when the death penalty and military conscription (compulsory National Service for young people to inculcate discipline) had been abolished, same-sex activity and relationships (albeit not marriage) had been legalized, abortion and divorce laws had been liberalized, and the contraceptive pill had been made available, via the NHS, to *all* women (having initially been issued only to married women).

During the 1970s, many on the right became alarmed at the marked increase in the number of divorces, the growing number of single or lone parents (some of whom had never been married, and were sometimes wholly reliant on welfare benefits until their children reached adulthood), the spread of sexually-transmitted diseases, the propensity of more young couples to live together ("in sin", as it was disapprovingly referred to) without getting married, and concomitantly, the extent to which the previous moral precept of no sex before marriage (especially for women, who were widely expected to be virgin brides) was derided and ignored by younger people, with many younger women insisting on the same sexual freedom and enjoyment that men had always experienced.

The growing apprehension which the right felt at these trends was compounded by other social developments and problems in the 1970s, most notably juvenile or adolescent delinquency, higher rates (and new types) of crime, football hooligans, punk rock(ers), and the growing number of television programmes and cinema films which featured swearing, blasphemy, nudity, sex scenes and/or violence, and which were widely considered shocking or pornographic at that time, but would probably be considered relatively mild today.

An additional concern was increasing welfare dependency and the apparent decline of the work ethic due to the availability of supposedly generous social security benefits; so-called welfare scroungers and the work-shy became targets of hostility on the right and in pro-Conservative newspapers – as remains the case today. According to Sherman: "Moral relativism had become ensconced. There were growing illegitimacy rates, welfare motherhood on an ever-expanding scale, children and teenagers running wild, the drug culture, increased crime, low clear-up rates, etc" (Sherman 2005: 69).

Whilst Thatcherism called for the state to be rolled back in the economic sphere, and people thereby granted the freedom to choose how to live their lives and spend their money, the opposite was demanded in the social and moral spheres, where the emphasis was on restoring law and order, reviving traditional morality – what Thatcher herself subsequently eulogized as "Victorian values" (TF 1983) – and tackling welfare dependency. All these objectives would entail a rolling forward of the state, closer regulation of some people's lives, and promotion of conformity of lifestyles. However, Thatcherites reasoned that those deemed responsible for these social and moral problems were usually unpopular minorities, such that the much-vaunted silent majority of the population would welcome an enhanced role for the state in imposing discipline and compliance on the alleged deviants and delinquents deemed responsible for social disorder and moral depravity. Herein we can discern the roots of Thatcherism's authoritarian populism, appealing to the anxieties and grievances of the supposedly decent, hard-working, law-abiding, tax-paying population by "othering" minorities and depicting them as internal enemies who constituted a threat to decency, morality and social stability, and whose freedoms and liberties were thus deemed rather less sacrosanct than those of apparently ordinary, decent, people.

This perspective was neatly encapsulated by Peregrine Worsthorne (while he was associate editor of the *Sunday Telegraph*) who was more concerned about restoring authority, order and traditional morality than promoting free-market economics and individual liberty. In an essay titled "Too Much Freedom", published a year before Thatcher became prime minister, he claimed that:

> Social discipline – that surely is a more fruitful and [re]warding theme for contemporary conservatism than individual freedom … The spectre haunting most ordinary people in

Britain is neither of a totalitarian state nor of Big Brother, but of other ordinary people being allowed to run wild. What they are worried about is crime, violence, disorder in the schools, promiscuity, idleness, pornography, football hooliganism, vandalism and urban terrorism … What Britain is suffering from is riotous disorder … The urgent need today is for the state to regain control over 'the people', to re-exert its authority, and it is useless to imagine that this will be helped by some libertarian mish-mash drawn from the writings of Adam Smith, John Stuart Mill, and the warmed-up milk of nineteenth-century liberalism. (Worsthorne 1978: 150, 149)

Whereas Worsthorne clearly prioritized the restoration of social discipline and traditional morality over the revival of free-market economics, many others associated with the development of Thatcherism viewed social discipline and economic liberalism as inextricably interlinked; they were not either/or alternatives or binary opposites, but wholly complementary and mutually reinforcing. Their reasoning was that the former was necessary to provide the moral framework and values necessary to support and sustain the essential features of the latter, namely entrepreneurship, enterprise, hard work, individual responsibility, self-reliance and wealth creation.

Thus did Alfred Sherman dismiss the economic liberal's utopian belief that if only restrictions on the market's operation were removed, a free society would burgeon, arguing instead that "a market economy is a necessary but not sufficient condition". This was because "for a market to flourish, many other moral and social pre-requisites were essential". In other words, it was necessary to ensure that the "social framework appropriate to economic stability and growth" was securely established (Sherman 2005: 56). This perspective was incorporated by Sherman into a 1974 speech he co-wrote with Keith Joseph, which reiterated that:

The economic situation is not an independent variable; it reflects the state of political life … the family and civilised values … are the foundation on which the nation is built; they are being undermined. If we cannot restore them to health, our nation can be utterly ruined – whatever economic policies we might try to follow. For economics is deeply shaped by values, by the attitude towards work, thrift, ethics, public-spirit … You will only have a healthy economy in a sound body politic. (TF 1974)

A similar observation had been expressed a few years earlier by Rhodes Boyson, a former teacher and headmaster, and later a junior minister in the Thatcher governments, who was renowned for his socially authoritarian views, and also instantly recognizable due to his carefully cultivated appearance of a strict and God-fearing Victorian schoolmaster or mill-owner, replete with prominent mutton-chop sideburns (Cockett 1995: 176; Markeson 2012). He lamented that:

> The moral fibre of our people has been weakened. A state which does for its citizens what they can do for themselves is an evil state; and a state which removes all choice and responsibility from its people … will create the irresponsible society. In such an irresponsible society, no-one cares, no-one saves, no-one bothers – why should they when the state spends all its energies taking money from the energetic, successful and thrifty to give to the idle, the failures and the feckless? … National economic strength and personal moral fibre are both reduced … We have been heading for economic and moral bankruptcy. (Boyson 1971: 5, 3, 7)

Herein lay clues to the eclectic character of much of the subsequent media and electoral support for Thatcherism, for while some were attracted by the pledges to liberate the British people from increasing state regulation or control, particularly in the economic sphere, many others hankered for a restoration of authority, conformism, discipline, social order and traditional morality. Of course, many voters, discerning no contradiction or tension between the two, wanted both; more freedom *and* more order. However, what this often meant was that they wanted for liberty for themselves, in terms of being able to buy their own home, enjoying more choice in buying goods and services, keeping more of the money they earned, owning shares, and generally going about their legitimate day-to-day activities or business without being impeded or inconvenienced by the disreputable behaviour or disruptive conduct of others. At the same time, however, these voters wanted the state to impose restrictions or punitive measures on others, most notably criminals, immigrants, protesters, trade unions, (young) unmarried mothers, and "work-shy" welfare recipients.

Why the postwar Conservative Party had failed to pursue "true" Conservatism

The vision of true Conservatism which Thatcherites developed from 1975 onwards was clearly very different to the ethos and policies which Conservative governments had subscribed to since 1945, except for the first two years of the Heath government. To the obvious question of why the pre-Thatcher Conservative Party had abandoned this supposed true Conservatism, Thatcherites offered five explanations.

The first was that postwar Britain had been characterized by a "ratchet effect", a concept advanced by Keith Joseph (Joseph 1976: 20–21; see also Joseph 1975: 6). He argued that the Conservative Party had taken its name too literally by accepting *a priori* that the role of Conservatism was merely to conserve, rather than advance its own distinct policy agenda. This was partly attributed to the party's professed eschewal of ideology, and thus its rejection of transformative or teleological blueprints. This meant that when post-1945 Conservative governments had been elected, they failed to repeal the supposedly left-wing policies of the defeated Labour government, and instead merely consolidated the status quo accordance with the "conservative" principles of continuity, harmony and stability. Consequently, Joseph claimed that:

> Since the end of the Second World War, we have had altogether too much Socialism … Conservative governments … did not consider it practicable to reverse the vast bulk of the accumulating detritus of Socialism which on each occasion they found when they returned to office … We are now more Socialist in many ways than any other developed country outside the Communist bloc – in the size of the public sector, the range of controls, and the telescoping of net income. (Joseph 1975: 6)

Thatcher naturally concurred, suggesting that "one of the reasons for our electoral failure is that people believe too many Conservatives have become socialists already" (Thatcher 1975). Thus did Thatcher inform the Conservative Philosophy Group, sometime in the mid-1970s (no-one seems aware of the actual date), that: "We must have an ideology. The other side have got an ideology ... we must have one too" (quoted in Young 1990: 406; Gilmour 1992: 6).

The second reason advanced by Thatcherites to explain their party's alleged abandonment of true Conservatism since 1945 was the character and temperament of many of the people who had dominated the Conservative Party since 1945, namely One Nation Conservatives, who were generally comfortable with the policy framework bequeathed by the 1945–51 Labour governments; a mixed economy containing key utilities in public ownership, a publicly-funded welfare state, the maintenance of full employment, and a conciliatory relationship with the trade unions. To this mix, in the 1960s, was added indicative economic planning, the incorporation of the trade unions into national-level discussions alongside employers' leaders and ministers via the National Economic Development Council (established in 1962), and governmental determination of wages via incomes policies.

Although there were occasional doubts and demurrals over the details of some of these policies, there was a broad acceptance among many senior Conservatives (the neoliberal Enoch Powell was a notable exception), not least because they generally seemed compatible with "the middle way" which Harold Macmillan (1938) had extolled just before the start of the Second World War; a middle way between laissez-faire capitalism and state socialism – neither Adam Smith nor Karl Marx.

The third reason, Thatcherites argued, why post-1945 Conservatives had failed to resist the steady drift leftwards in economic and social affairs was that most public institutions had been colonized by liberals and the left – the right tend to conflate the two, and treat them as synonymous, probably because both view themselves as progressive and thus anti-Conservative. Consequently, whereas pre- or non-Thatcherite Conservatives had been strongly committed to the defence of established institutions – which were deemed both to enshrine accumulated wisdom and practical experience, and provide a major source of continuity and stability by linking the past to the present and the future – Thatcherites were characterized by their increasing suspicion of, or even hostility to, institutions such as the BBC, civil service, local government, schools, social services, and universities, and those who worked in these public bodies. This, in turn, became one of the contradictions of Thatcherism and its increasingly unconservative praxis, which we return to in the final chapter.

For Thatcherites, the alleged colonization of such institutions and professions by liberals and the left had two deleterious consequences. The first was that of agenda-setting, whereby anti-Conservative views and values had strongly shaped the ethos or in-house ideology of these institutions, and through them, permeated much of British society. To the obvious question of how the Conservative Party succeeded in winning general elections in 1951, 1955, 1959 and 1970 in the face of this alleged anti-Conservative influence, the Thatcherites would respond that postwar Conservative governments were effectively constrained in the policies they could propose and enact, due to the hegemony of liberals and the left in these institutions, and the extent to which they both shaped the organizational agenda, and the terms of debate (including what was deemed feasible or necessary) or discourse, and their practical impact on policies.

For example, Thatcher partly attributed increased criminality and juvenile delinquency to "the fashionable theories and permissive claptrap" which apparently prevailed among "the professional progressives among broadcasters, social workers and politicians who have created a fog of excuses in which the mugger and the burglar operate" (quoted in *The Observer*, 28 March 1982 and *The Independent*, 21 March 1988). Moreover, Thatcherites were convinced that too many postwar Conservative ministers had readily accepted much of the ideological agenda and concomitant arguments of cultural, political and social institutions, due to the party's pre-Thatcherite commitment to consensus, continuity, pragmatism (as a principle, rather than a tactic) and social stability.

Thatcherites also condemned the prominent role which this consensual mode of governance granted to senior public sector workers or their representatives via policy communities, and the emphasis on negotiation and mutual agreement when any changes were proposed (Jordan & Richardson 1982; Marsh & Rhodes 1992). This was because such a mode of governance constituted a surrendering of political authority to unelected bureaucrats and unaccountable professionals, who were thus able simultaneously to prioritize their own interests over those of the people they were supposed to serve, and promote their liberal or left-wing values over the supposedly common-sense views of most British people. This was deemed a major reason Britain had apparently suffered from an anti-enterprise or anti-business culture since the 1960s. Thatcher thus lamented "a consistent tendency in our society to denigrate the creators of wealth. Nowhere is this attitude more marked than in cloister and common room" (quoted in *The Observer*, 24 March 1985).

A fourth, but closely related, reason advanced by Thatcherites to explain the post-1945 expansion of the state was the aforementioned colonization of key public sector institutions, including local government, by professionals whose careers, prestige and status were enhanced by the extent to which they could annually acquire more resources, and sometimes more bureaucratic power, which in turn strengthened their leverage over elected politicians. Whereas competition in the private sector was motivated by the imperative of attracting more customers to increase profits and thus commercial success, Thatcherites lamented that the only competition or incentive which seemed to exist in the public sector was the relentless demand of each service or institution to maximize its own budget, and persuade the relevant minister or, ultimately, the Treasury, that it could only improve service provision if it was permitted to recruit more staff; the NHS routinely argued for more doctors and nurses, schools constantly insisted that they needed to employ more teachers, and social services always pleaded for more social workers. More generally, Maurice Cowling lamented the era of supposedly self-serving progressive causes which either sought more funding and/or demanded more governmental action: "the age of the welfare worker, the liberal bishop, the race-relations and third-World industries, and the counter-cultures embodied in the Green Movement, the Feminist Movement" (Cowling 1990: xlv).

This perspective also revealed the influence on Thatcherism of public choice theory, a pro-market perspective mainly developed by some academics and economists in the United States from the 1960s onwards, but which strongly complemented the neoliberal aspects of Thatcherism, and the critique of how and why the state and public sector had expanded relentlessly. Public choice theorists attributed much of the expansion of the state and public services, and the inexorable increase in funding, to the pursuit of budget-maximization, bureaucratic empire-building, and professional self-interest by supposedly altruistic civil servants and street-level bureaucrats in the public sector (see, e.g., Buchanan & Tullock 1962; Lee 2012; Niskanen 1971; Tullock, Seldon & Brady 2000). From this perspective, many public sector workers were knaves rather than knights (Le Grand 2003: ch. 2), and consequently, ever-increasing funding and expansion of staff did not yield a corresponding increase or improvement in service provision for the wider population and taxpayers.

For example, it was suggested that a key problem in higher education was that universities "are producer, not consumer, driven institutions. They are run in the interests of staff ... not in the interests of students who, as consumers, face a classic cartel" (NA 1986a). The same criticism was made of secondary education, which, it was lamented, still effectively operated as a nationalized industry more than six years after the election of the first Thatcher government. Consequently, "the provider decides what the customer ought to have, largely ignoring what the customer actually wants ... and every problem is attributed to a shortage of public subsidy" (NA 1986b). Thatcher also bemoaned that the Department of Education (DES) had "become closely connected with its clients ... in particular the National Union of Teachers (NUT)" to the extent that "a large number of DES senior civil servants ... and the NUT leaders were on the closest terms ... a common sympathy" (Thatcher 1995: 166).

The fifth reason cited by Thatcherites to explain why their Conservative predecessors had failed to resist the steady drift leftwards in economic and social affairs, and the concomitant increase in state intervention, was fear of the anticipated electoral consequences of refusing to increase public spending and expand the provision of purportedly free services. According to some Thatcherites, electoral competition unwittingly encouraged political irresponsibility, as parties competed for votes in general elections partly by pledging to increase public spending and expand the provision of services at a higher or faster rate than their rivals: "parliamentary democracy has an inbuilt tendency towards excessive expenditure" (Sherman 2005: 65).

This phenomenon had been identified by the *Financial Times* journalist and author, Samuel Brittan, as one of "the economic contradictions of democracy", whereby competing politicians and parties promised ever-increasing state spending in order to attract votes. However, in so doing, he argued that they unwittingly weakened, and ultimately destroyed, the economic conditions which capitalism needed to flourish and generate the wealth on which jobs and prosperity heavily depended, while also providing the tax revenues necessary to fund the promised or improved public services (Brittan 1975a, 1975b). According to Sherman (2005: 71): "The auction of promises seemed to legitimise itself, and politicians dared not question it for fear of being accused of callousness and ... losing elections", a scenario which Brittan termed "the Wenceslas myth" (Brittan 1983: ch. 1). In effect, political democracy and short-term electoralism were killing the economic goose which laid the golden egg.

However, Thatcherites (and various other critics) argued that there was a further political problem which accrued from the state's increasing role in providing ostensibly free public services and tackling socio-economic problems, namely that the more it intervened, the more it attracted demands from citizens and organized interests who believed that their problems or interests were not being acknowledged or addressed, or who complained that someone else was receiving preferential treatment. This placed additional demands on politicians which ultimately threatened to overwhelm governments, particularly as responding favourably to the lobbying of one section of society might conflict with the interests of another. Governments faced a potential no-win situation, condemned by some if they did *not* intervene to tackle a grievance or problem, but equally liable to attract criticism from others if they did; the ineluctable result was the "overload of government", and ultimately, a steady loss of political authority and legitimacy (King 1975).

The ideas and intellectual theories, developed in opposition by the key individuals and think tanks discussed above, provided the Conservative Party with an increasingly confident critique of how postwar British government had apparently pursued the wrong path, and dragged Britain ever closer towards Soviet-style state control and planning. Yet to the emerging Thatcherites, the blame did not rest solely with the Labour Party, because the Conservative Party's One Nation cohort were also deemed culpable, having failed to reverse and repeal many of Labour's policies when the Conservatives were in government; they had merely sought to conserve and maintain the status quo.

However, regardless of how inherently and internally logical political ideas are, they will rarely acquire wider acceptance or influence unless they provide a coherent and convincing explanation of contemporary empirical events; they need to correspond to circumstances, and thereby provide a plausible explanation of what many ordinary citizens are experiencing, while also offering credible policy solutions. As one of Britain's most eminent and prolific political historians and biographers notes: "Ideas, to be successfully taken up, need advocates (individuals or interests), they need to square with the facts ... and be launched in positive circumstances" (Seldon 1996: 289).

Or as the American political scientist, John Kingdon (1984: *passim*) argues, policy change usually requires the confluence of three metaphorical streams: the problem stream, the policy stream and the political stream. This means that: a problem is acknowledged, and deemed serious or disruptive enough to warrant political action; a policy is available to address the problem – this can be a policy formulated directly in response to the problem, or it can be a policy which "policy entrepreneurs" (such as ideologically-motivated individuals or think tanks) have long cherished and canvassed, and now present as the ready-made solution to the new problem; the appropriate political circumstances exist for the policy to be enacted, such as a new government claiming an electoral mandate, a particular faction dominant in the governing party, a favourable shift in public opinion, lack of effective political opposition, or the severity (real or perceived) of a crisis facing a country at a particular juncture.

The ideas which subsequently constituted Thatcherism certainly had some enthusiastic advocates, but as noted in the previous chapter, before the winter of discontent, many voters seemed unconvinced, or were hesitant about supporting a radical departure from the status quo, despite their growing concern about crime, immigration, strikes and welfare dependency. In terms of Kingdon's three policy streams, the problems were recognized, and several policies were developed or presented as solutions, but electorally and politically, the circumstances were not yet appropriate.

In this context, it was the 1978–79 winter of discontent which imbued nascent Thatcherism with greater public credence, for it seemed to exemplify with much of what the Conservative right and allied newspapers had been arguing about nationalized industries, the public sector and trade union militancy. Enough voters were finally persuaded that persevering with the extant policies was no longer tenable or desirable.

In effect, the third stream identified by Kingdon now merged with the problem and policy stream, as circumstances and the political situation changed sufficiently to establish the conditions in which the new policies could now be introduced. As Milton Friedman (1982: iv) later observed: "Only a crisis – actual or perceived – produces real change. When that crisis occurs, the actions that are taken depend on the ideas that are lying around. That, I believe, is our basic function: to develop alternatives to existing policies, to keep them alive and available until the politically impossible becomes the politically inevitable".

This reinforces the earlier point about policy advocates or policy entrepreneurs, who not only promote particular policies because they support them intellectually or ideologically, but who look for, or even define, problems for which their policy preference(s) will provide the solution. They then seek to persuade the media, policy-makers, party leaders and governments that a particular policy will tackle a specific problem. However, unless political circumstances are conducive, or a serious crisis emerges to persuade politicians that fundamental change is unavoidably necessary, then the ideas and policies canvassed by these policy entrepreneurs are unlikely to be adopted and implemented; they will remain confined to the pages of think tank pamphlets or academic journals, or in-house conferences and seminars attended mainly by fellow believers.

In the case of Thatcherism, the winter of discontent crystallized and legitimized many of the arguments, critiques, policies and theories which had previously been promoted by intellectuals and theorists such as Milton Friedman, Friedrich Hayek, Enoch Powell, Alfred Sherman and Norman Strauss, the American public choice school of economists personified by Gordon Tullock and William Niskanen, and think tanks such as the Centre for Policy Studies and the Institute of Economic Affairs. Some of these policy entrepreneurs had been promoting their ideas and theories since the 1940s, 1950s or 1960s, but it was not until the late 1970s, in the context of the economic, industrial, political and social problems facing Britain, that enough senior Conservative politicians became fully persuaded by their arguments and associated policy solutions.

3

The key policies

The manifesto on which the first Thatcher government was elected in 1979 was a relatively modest document compared to the radicalism which followed as the 1980s progressed, but nonetheless, it was clear that a significant change of ideological direction was envisaged, as delineated in the previous chapter, which entailed new political priorities and policies. Although there were clear pledges on cutting direct taxation and selling council houses to their tenants, on many other flagship Thatcherite policies, such as privatization, and trade union reform, the 1979 manifesto was rather restrained in what it promised. There were four reasons for this modesty, the first being that election manifestos aim to present voters with a political party's overall objectives and priorities, albeit including a few attractive policy pledges, rather than a detailed itinerary of every proposed measure and legislation.

Second, the inclusion of too many specific or detailed policy pledges might alienate some potential voters, either because they might dislike some of the pledged policies, or because the more detail provided, the more political ammunition this will provide to the party's rivals, who will then seek to frighten voters about the implications of a particular policy, and how it will detrimentally affect them.

The third reason for the relative opacity of the Conservatives 1979 manifesto was that the party was itself ideologically divided between Thatcherites and One Nation Conservatives, or "dries and wets" in common parlance, and hence the manifesto reflected the need for compromise by only offering pledges and policies that both philosophical wings of the party could endorse; more contentious or controversial policy proposals needed to be omitted or toned down.

Fourth, Thatcher herself was not yet sufficiently confident about how radical she and a Conservative government could be. As we noted in the previous chapter, she had many ideas and instincts about what she wanted to change and achieve, but was unsure about how far, or how fast, she would be able to implement the policies and reforms which she favoured. Consequently, some Thatcherite policies were pursued incrementally, while others were not enacted until the latter years of her premiership, by which time her confidence (along with that of her closest ministerial colleagues) had increased, and sources of opposition – both inside the Conservative Party and far beyond – had been weakened.

Public expenditure

The reduction of public expenditure was a key Thatcherite goal from the late 1970s onwards, and integral to the multiple objectives of curbing the money supply to reduce inflation, rolling back the state to enable entrepreneurs and the private sector to flourish, promoting much greater individual liberty and choice for consumers, and yielding financial savings which could then fund cuts in direct taxation. As Dennis Kavanagh (1987: 225) explained, Thatcherites envisaged that "by curbing the growth in public spending they would create the headroom for tax reductions which in turn [would] provide incentives and liberate the entrepreneurial energies of the British people".

The goal of lower public expenditure was to be achieved in several ways:

- Adopting a monetarist policy of strictly controlling or curbing the money supply to reduce inflation, this control to be achieved via strict limits on public expenditure by governments, and the adjustment of interest rates charged on borrowing; in the case of the latter, if inflation increased, interest rates would also be raised, clearly making borrowing more expensive. The expectation and intention was that borrowing would diminish, thus reducing consumer spending or demand for goods, and ultimately result in lower inflation as prices stabilized, or even fell. The downside was that unemployment would increase markedly when firms sell less, profits decline, and bankruptcies ensue.
- Abandoning Keynesianism, whereupon economic growth and employment would no longer be pursued directly via higher

government spending and investment, but through supply-side economics and creating the optimal conditions in which entrepreneurs and the private sector could flourish, free from political direction and regulation.

- Transferring state-owned industries to the private sector, thus relinquishing financial responsibility for them in terms of annual subsidies and staff remuneration.
- Imposing strict cash limits on the public sector (including local government), and in some instances, redundancies or/and leaving job vacancies unfilled, so that they would be compelled to become much more careful and efficient in how they spent their budgets; doing more with less.
- Increase public sector pay by less than the rate of inflation.
- Defer capital (infrastructure) spending; it was deemed relatively easy to delay the resurfacing of a motorway, or the building of a new prison or maternity unit, for another year or two.
- Reduce the size of the civil service, thereby cutting the annual cost of salaries to be funded by the Treasury, while simultaneously cutting state bureaucracy and red tape.
- Contract-out sundry public services or functions to the private sector, on the basis that this would enable them to be performed or provided more cheaply: for example, school dinners and hospital cleaning.
- Reform and restructure the welfare state to reduce eligibility for social security benefits, impose a much stricter regime on "undeserving" claimants, namely the unemployed and single parents, and strictly limit the annual rate of increase in the value of social security benefits.

In practice, the Thatcher governments found it virtually impossible to reduce overall public expenditure in terms of the actual cash amount spent, due to such factors as inflation and higher costs generally, and the need to increase wages and welfare benefits (albeit at a lower or slower rate than previously). Moreover, some of the political priorities of Thatcherism itself entailed increases in government spending, such as strengthening defence policy via upgrading nuclear weaponry, and increasing law and order via more police and prisons. It was also the case that some policies had repercussions on others; for example,

Thatcherism's economic policies resulted in increasing unemployment, which meant that the overall amount spent on social security increased, regardless of the curbs on welfare benefits paid to individual claimants.

Consequently, during Thatcher's premiership, total public expenditure actually increased from £93 billion in 1979–80 to £210 billion in 1989–90 (Rogers 2013). When ministers talked about cutting public expenditure, what they usually meant was two things: slowing down the rate at which government spending increased compared to previous decades, and reducing it as a proportion of GDP or national wealth. The latter meant that if the economy grew by 2 per cent, but public expenditure only increased by 1 per cent in any year, for example, ministers could simultaneously boast that they were spending more "in cash terms" on education or health care, but reducing the share of national wealth (GDP) consumed by public expenditure. Thus, for example, although public spending in actual cash terms more than doubled during Thatcher's premiership, it also declined as a proportion of GDP, from 44 per cent to 39 per cent. Hence the Thatcher premiership witnessed both a doubling and a significant reduction of public spending, depending on what criteria or measurement was used.

Taxation

During Thatcher's premiership, "cutting taxation" became a prime objective for many Conservatives, in tandem with the parallel pledge to reduce the tax burden – the tendency of many Conservatives to view tax as a "burden", rather than the price of living in a civilized society, is itself highly significant ideologically. As noted in Chapter 2, Thatcherites not only believed that income tax was far too high, especially on the wealthy, but that income tax was, in effect, a necessary evil which should be minimized as far as practicably possible. Britain's allegedly punitive rates of income tax prior to the election of the first Thatcher government were deemed to be a disincentive to hard work in general, and entrepreneurship and wealth creation in particular. This, in turn, meant that the level of direct taxation was one of the obstacles to the neoliberal economic revolution which Thatcherism was determined to pursue.

Thus did chancellor Geoffrey Howe, in his first Budget, in June 1979, cut the top rate of income tax from 83 per cent to 60 per cent, and the basic rate from 33 per cent to 30 per cent. These were subsequently reduced to 40 per cent and 25 per cent respectively in 1988, when Nigel Lawson was chancellor. However, the 1979 income tax cut was offset by the near doubling of value added tax (VAT), from 8 per cent to 15 per cent, which meant that for many people on lower incomes, their total annual tax payments hardly decreased; what they gained from income tax cuts was offset by the increase in VAT payments (and also higher national insurance contributions during the 1980s). This is because VAT is a regressive tax, meaning that it disproportionately affects the poorer sections of British society. It is a tax paid on a purchased item or service, and is therefore not linked to earnings or income: if £100 VAT is payable on an item, then everyone who buys it will have to pay the £100 "indirect" tax, but that effectively constitutes a much larger payment for a worker on the minimum wage or a pensioner than it does for a millionaire. Consequently, during Thatcher's premiership, overall taxation, measured as a proportion of GDP, increased from 38.8 per cent in 1979 to 39.3 per cent in 1990 (Jackson & Saunders 2012). Moreover, the poorest 20 per cent of the population were contributing 40 per cent of their incomes to the Treasury, whereas the wealthiest 20 per cent contributed only 35 per cent (Garnett & Gilmour 1996: 85).

Due to the combined impact of enormous income tax cuts on high salaries, and the exponential increase of pay in Britain's company boardrooms and the City, during the Thatcher premiership, the rich became very much richer (and have continued to do so ever since). Their pay and wealth increased at a much faster and higher rate than the incomes of ordinary workers, which in turn meant that Thatcherism became synonymous with greatly increased inequality, and a growing gulf between the richest and the poorest in British society (Dorling 2018; Dorey 2015b; Goodman, Johnson & Webb 1997; Mount 2012). However, anyone who sought to highlight this growing gulf between the richest and the poorest was variously accused of fomenting the policy of envy, of being a crypto-communist, or of wanting to make everyone exactly the same. Similar allegations are made today against anyone who criticizes the continuing increase in socio-economic inequality, and the multi-million-pound salaries routinely paid in many corporate boardrooms in the City.

Privatization

The best example of a Thatcherite policy which commenced cautiously, but later became more ambitious and radical was privatization, whereby nationalized, or state-owned, industries were transferred to private ownership through the selling of shares. Crucially, some of these shares were sold directly to ordinary people, rather than to the stock market and existing institutional shareholders. Although it became a flagship policy of the Thatcher governments, privatization initially entailed the sale of smaller state-owned firms such as British Petroleum, British Aerospace, Cable & Wireless, and the National Freight Company, but these were transferred to the private sector via the selling of shares to already established corporate investors, companies and pension funds.

At this stage, in the early 1980s, ministers had not realized the full potential or practical feasibility of selling shares directly to the British public. As Norman Tebbit, a staunch ideological ally and cabinet colleague of Thatcher, subsequently explained, "few Conservatives believed it could be achieved on such a scale and to such an extent", while fellow Thatcherite Nicholas Ridley recalled that "we learned how to do it with the smaller ones", and when these "early sales proved an undoubted success, we not only felt emboldened enough to proceed with the bigger ones, but we knew how to do it" (Tebbit 1991: 27–8; Ridley 1991: 60). Or as Thatcher herself reflected, after the initial small-scale privatizations during her first government, "we got bolder, and we learned as we went along" (Thatcher 1995: 574). The biggest and thus most significant privatizations occurred from 1984 onwards, starting with British Telecom, followed by British Gas in 1986, British Airways in 1987, British Steel in 1988, the water companies in 1989, and the electricity industry in 1990.

A variety of motives were cited by ministers to justify these sales, the main ones being to reduce public expenditure (by transferring heavily subsidized, non-profit-making, state-owned industries and their wage bill to the private sector), break-up inefficient monopolies, and promote greater competition within each industry or sector, which would then provide consumers and customers with more choice, a higher standard of service and lower costs. The Thatcherite premise was that in competing to attract more customers, and thus boost profits and maximize shareholder value, privatized companies would constantly need to offer the public higher quality services and/or lower prices; if they failed to do so, their customers would switch to another service provider, something which they could not do under the former regime of state-owned monopolies. In this regard, privatization was meant to promote what Thatcherites termed consumer sovereignty.

A further advantage of privatization envisaged by Thatcherites was that it would contribute to the weakening of trade unions, in two main ways. First, by breaking-up these industries into several companies, fragmented either on the basis of functions or regionalization (or both, as in the case of the railways), the unions would find it much more difficult to conduct a *national* strike causing the maximum of industrial disruption or public inconvenience, and which then placed intense pressure on governments to concede to union demands. For example, it was envisaged that if train drivers in Wales went on strike, then rail passengers in and around London and the South-east, or in Scotland, would experience little, if any, disruption. Second, it was envisaged that trade unions would realize that the jobs and wages of their members were now wholly dependent on the profitability of their company or industry, rather than government subsidies and bailouts. Indeed, a strike might sufficiently damage their company's profitability, or deter future investment, that redundancies would follow, meaning that workers who went on strike for higher pay might lose their jobs, and thus wages, altogether: for Thatcherites, workers needed to learn that low pay was better than no pay, and that in times of high unemployment especially, low-paid workers ought to be grateful that they had a job at all.

Apart from the size of the industries sold, there was another crucial difference between the early selloffs and those pursued after 1984, namely that the latter entailed selling shares directly to the public, often over the counter of their local high-street bank. Millions of people who had previously never owned shares were suddenly able to buy them without the need to hire a financial agent or stockbroker. Moreover, the Thatcher governments sold the shares at below their market value, in order to render them attractive and affordable to members of the public; if a merchant bank advised the Thatcher government that shares in a soon-to-be privatized company would be worth £5 each on the stock market, they would be sold to the public at, say, £2.50. Naturally, many people who bought shares did so with the sole intention of immediately selling them, thereby making a healthy and instant profit, and then using this additional money to buy a new car, conduct home improvements, or perhaps have a once-in-a-lifetime holiday. The Treasury itself conceded that by 1990, the number of shareholders in British Airways had fallen from over 1,000,000 to less than 350,000, whereas share ownership in British Gas fell from 4.4 million people in 1986 to 2.7 million four years later (HM Treasury 1990: 7; see also Abromeit 1988: 78).

Notwithstanding the number of people who soon sold their shares, the Thatcher governments anticipated that a major long-term political advantage would accrue from privatization, namely that wider share-ownership would pose serious problems for the Labour Party, which was then formally committed to (re-)nationalization. Thatcherites envisaged that many ordinary people who bought (and retained) shares in privatized industries were unlikely to vote Labour. This was a key reason why the Labour Party's Clause IV (which enshrined the party's formal commitment to public ownership of industries) was rewritten, in 1995, under Tony Blair's leadership, whereupon the party was rebranded *New* Labour. In 2002, Thatcher confessed that she considered Tony Blair and New Labour to have been her greatest achievement: "We forced our opponents to change their minds" (quoted in Burns 2008).

One other flagship Thatcherite policy, which simultaneously constituted a mode of privatization, and also a shrinkage of the welfare state, was the sale of council houses. Tenants were offered the opportunity to buy their houses and to become homeowners. To enhance the affordability of council properties, existing tenants were offered a discount on the purchase price; the longer they had been renting, the larger the discount. Between 1980, when the "right to buy" was enshrined in legislation, and the end of Thatcher's premiership in late 1990, one million local authority dwellings were sold to their tenants, significantly expanding homeownership, and probably also extending the Conservative Party's electoral base; homeowners usually being much more likely than renters to vote Conservative.

The right to buy additionally furthered the Thatcherite objectives of both reducing the role and scope of local government, and curbing public expenditure, especially as local authorities were not permitted to build new properties to replace those which were sold. The last point indicates Thatcher's determination to ensure that the market provided Britain's housing, either through homeownership, or private renting. For those who could not access or afford either of these, the main residual public or social housing was that provided by housing associations, and over time, even these were expected to charge market-based rents, which naturally rendered them more expensive. The legacy of these policies is one of the reasons for the shortage of affordable housing in Britain today, although this is an issue which has also been "racialized", as asylum seekers and immigrants are sometimes accused of causing or exacerbating the shortage of affordable housing – one of the factors underpinning support for the UK's withdrawal from the European Union (Brexit) in some left-behind communities (Shilliam 2018: ch. 6). Britain's housing crisis is an issue to which we return in Chapter 6, when we discuss some of the enduring but negative consequences of Thatcherism.

Trade union reform

Another key Thatcherite policy, albeit also pursued in a step-by-step manner and cumulatively resulting in a major and irreversible transformation over 11 years (and beyond), was the reform of trade unionism, and industrial relations more generally. For Thatcherites, curbing the power of the trade unions was essential to achieving the wider economic and industrial transformation that Britain was deemed to need. Instead of accepting the power of the trade unions as an unavoidable fact of life and thus pursuing dialogue or partnership with organized labour, as One Nation Tories strongly preferred, Thatcherites insisted that not only should trade union power and apparent privileges (in terms of their legal immunities) be steadily reduced, but that a Thatcher government should also be fully prepared for a major challenge from a strong trade union which would have to be defeated by deploying the full power and resources of the state.

The most obvious way in which the Thatcher governments irrevocably weakened the trade unions, and inter alia explicitly promoted both management's right to manage and what neoliberals term labour market flexibility, was through legislation. From 1980 to 1990, five laws were enacted, each of which imposed more obligations and restrictions on the trade unions, and cumulatively weakened their industrial power, namely, the requirement for secret ballots before embarking on industrial action, the election of trade union leaders, and to gauge members' support for their union operating a political fund; the narrowing of the definition of a trade dispute over which workers could legitimately go on strike; limiting the number of workers (to six) who could picket the entrance to a workplace during a strike (supposedly to prevent intimidation of strike-breakers or public disorder); outlawing the "closed shop", the system of compulsory union membership that had previously operated in some industries; and outlawing secondary or sympathy industrial action, meaning that strikes in solidarity with other workers were prohibited.

In addition to the actual content of these laws, four aspects are worth emphasizing. The first is that four of the (five) laws were titled Employment Acts, to emphasize the Thatcher governments' premise that the conduct of the trade unions was itself a significant cause of unemployment, due to the economic damage wrought by lost production, deterred investment and reduced profitability or even bankruptcies allegedly caused by excessive pay rises secured through strikes. Thatcherites thus argued that weakening the trade unions would generate new jobs and boost employment.

The second notable feature of the five trade union laws enacted was that defying them was classified as a civil, not criminal, offence, whereupon it was for aggrieved or affected individuals (employers, trade union members or other employees or customers) to instigate proceedings against trade unions which defied the law, rather than ministers themselves. This was intended to depoliticize industrial conflict by ensuring that government ministers were not directly dragged into industrial disputes or called upon to instigate legal action when the law was broken.

Also, by classifying breaches of trade union laws as civil offences, the Thatcher governments ensured that no trade unionists or leaders would be sent to prison for defiance; this would avoid the risk of unwittingly creating "martyrs" who might attract wider trade union support, and even public sympathy. As employment secretary from 1981 to 1983, Norman Tebbit explained to his senior civil servants that: "Under no circumstances will I allow any trade union activist – however hard he tries – to get himself into prison under my legislation" (Tebbit 1988:

182). Instead, unions who engaged in unlawful industrial action would be punished by having fines imposed on them, and if a trade union continually defied a judicial instruction to halt such action immediately, then it ultimately risked bankruptcy as the fines increased.

The third notable aspect of the Thatcher governments' trade union laws was their incremental enactment. This was a lesson learned from the 1971 Industrial Relations Act, which had sought to reform (curb) the trade unions in one all-encompassing piece of legislation, but in so doing, had provided the unions with a clear target against which to mobilize opposition and defiance. Instead, the Thatcher governments pursued trade union reform gradually, so that each law appeared relatively modest or innocuous, and built upon or consolidated previous legislation, but with the ultimate impact being far-reaching and practically irreversible (Dorey 2016b; see also Dorey 2003). This cautious approach made it virtually impossible for the unions to claim that they – and British workers – were being subjected to a draconian all-out political assault or vindictive attack by a right-wing Conservative government.

The fourth notable aspect of the Thatcher governments' reform of industrial relations and trade unionism was the manner in which it was presented as a means of empowering ordinary union members against their leaders. Ministers invoked terms like "handing the unions back to their members" and "democratising the trade unions" vis-à-vis supposedly politically-motivated union leaders who allegedly often relied on coercion and intimidation of union members to support strike action.

However, the power that was being granted to ordinary trade unionists vis-à-vis their union leaders was simultaneously being greatly reduced vis-à-vis their employers and workplace managers. In the name of management's right to manage and labour market flexibility, the 1980s saw the Thatcher governments steadily reduce employment protection and workers' rights, so that it became easier for employers to impose new – less favourable – working practices or hours of employment on their staff, by altering their terms and conditions of employment. It also became more difficult for workers to claim unfair dismissal.

Meanwhile, the first (1979–83) Thatcher government carefully prepared for a major confrontation with the coalminers, in accordance with a blueprint provided by the supposedly confidential 1978 (Nicholas) Ridley report. This had assumed that the next Conservative government was likely to face a serious challenge, in the form of a major strike, from a key trade union or powerful group of workers, quite possibly in response to planned closures and/or redundancies. It was therefore deemed essential that ministers were well prepared, so that they – and the country – could withstand, and ultimately defeat, such a confrontation. The Ridley report provided the first Thatcher government with a strategy to prepare for an anticipated strike by coalminers: building-up coal reserves by offering miners generous overtime deals, recruiting non-union lorry drivers, deploying police officers from other parts of the country, for example. Then, when fully prepared, it could provoke, and ultimately defeat, a strike, which is exactly what the second Thatcher government did when the National Union of Mineworkers (NUM) embarked upon a year-long strike against pit closures and redundancies in 1984–85. Some miners did not support this industrial action and continued working, whereupon they were strongly praised for their courage by Conservative ministers, for whom these working miners were integral to defeating the NUM and its controversial leader, Arthur Scargill (Dorey 2013). Needless to say, little more was heard from ministers about these miners' apparent right to work when their pits were subsequently closed, and they too were made redundant; they had served their political purpose.

A final, more general, way in which the trade unions were weakened under the Thatcher governments was by excluding them from regular discussions and decision-taking with ministers. Whereas previous Conservative governments had often sought to foster cooperation and partnership with trade union leaders, most notably through the National Economic Development Council (NEDC), which had been established in 1962 by Macmillan's Conservative government, Thatcherites had no desire for such collaboration, nor did they see any necessity for dialogue with the unions. Quite apart from Thatcherism's innate ideological hostility towards the trade unions, such partnership was viewed as a redundant relic of the previous era based on consensus politics and close governmental involvement in industrial and economic affairs. Hence Lord Young's boast that: "We have rejected the TUC; we have rejected the CBI. We do not see them coming back again. We gave up the corporate state" (*Financial Times*, 9 November 1988). This was another example of Thatcher's conviction politics and emphatic rejection of consensus.

Rejecting incomes policies

As we noted in the previous chapter, Thatcherism rejected the hitherto assumption that inflation was a consequence of wage increases fuelling price rises and thus a higher cost of living. Once Thatcherites accepted that inflation was ultimately derived from supposedly excessive increases in the money supply, unmatched by higher industrial productivity or faster economic growth, then incomes policies became irrelevant as a method of economic management (Dorey 2001: ch. 7). The main consequence of trade unions pursuing "excessive" wage rises would be higher unemployment as their employer became unprofitable, leading to bankruptcy and redundancies.

As such, it was deemed either to be the responsibility of employers to resist unaffordable pay claims, or of the unions themselves to be more responsible when seeking higher wages for their members via free collective bargaining. It was not deemed to be the role of ministers to rescue employers or trade unionists from the consequences of their own alleged irresponsibility in the sphere of pay determination. Nor was it the state's role to determine what constituted a fair or reasonable wage, or how much should be paid to tackle poverty; these were subjective social and political questions, whereas Thatcherites considered pay to be a purely objective economic issue determined by the free market, whereupon wages and salaries would be determined in the context of commercial criteria: what a company could afford to pay in terms of profitability, and what remuneration it needed to offer to recruit or retain workers with the requisite skills.

The rejection of incomes policies – notwithstanding continued governmental responsibility for determining pay, via cash limits, in the public sector – would greatly reduce the likelihood of ministers becoming embroiled in wage negotiations or disputes, and this, in turn, would serve to restore the autonomy and authority of governments and the state.

Reforming the public sector

The reform or modernization of the public sector was derived both from the Thatcherite commitment to curbing public expenditure, with education and the NHS constituting two of the three largest spheres of government spending (the other being social security), and the ideological conviction that the private sector was inherently more efficient, cost-effective and responsive to consumers, than monopolistic public services which were funded via taxation. However, even Thatcherites baulked at directly privatizing hospitals, schools and universities, for administrative, electoral, logistical and practical reasons. Instead, public sector reform entailed two strategies to render such services more business-like, cost-effective and responsive to their customers and clients, namely marketization and managerialism.

Marketization

This entailed either imitating, or wherever possible, incorporating, private sector principles and practices into public sector services like education, healthcare, the probation service and social services. Thatcherism deemed such services to have an innate proclivity to inefficiency, partly due to lack of competition, which meant that those who relied on them could not go elsewhere to an alternative provider; they were a captive clientele. In this context, those who worked in the public sector had little incentive to offer a more courteous or efficient service to retain their current customers, and/or attract new ones.

However, the alleged inefficiency was also attributed to the funding of the public sector, which relied heavily or wholly on central or local government for the annual allocation of funds. Thatcherism believed that if public sector workers complacently assumed that politicians would regularly allocate the necessary funds each year, then doctors, nurses, probation officers, social workers, teachers and university lecturers would have little or no incentive to work harder, or improve the quality of the service they provided, either to their clients, or taxpayers in general. This contrasted starkly with the private sector, where providing a poor service would ultimately result in fewer customers, declining sales, diminishing profits and eventual job losses.

A further reason why Thatcherites deemed the public sector to provide a much less efficient service than the private sector was, as discussed in the previous chapter, the phenomenon of "producer capture", whereby many front-line or public-facing professionals supposedly prioritized their individual or institutional interests over those of their clients. Instead of public sector professionals being motivated by altruism, philanthropy, and a genuine commitment to serving the community or society (or disadvantaged sections within it), Thatcherites viewed many of them as self-serving budget-maximizers, bureaucratic empire-builders and sectional vested interests. The Thatcher governments were therefore committed to changing how the public sector was funded and functioned, and transforming the culture of those employed within it.

The process of marketization entailed several measures to render the public sector more business-like. Firstly, by establishing internal markets inside specific sectors or services, such as the "purchaser vs provider" distinction in the NHS, whereby GPs (local doctors) were designated purchasers, with an annual budget, who "bought" a package of treatment (such as surgery) from whichever hospital they considered to be the best. This was intended to compel hospitals to compete for contracts from local GPs, and thereby imitate the competition for customers that private companies engage in on a constant basis. Seconsly, by linking at least some funding to the outputs or outcomes achieved by public services, either by attracting more customers or clients (due the quality of served provided) or attaining politically or ministerially specified performance indicators or targets. This was intended to imitate the profit motive of the private sector, where more customers usually mean more institutional income and a larger financial surplus. Thirdly, by "contracting-out" various public sector activities to private companies, such as cleaning and catering in schools and hospitals. The assumption was that such services would normally be provided more cheaply or cost-effectively by a private company than being performed "in-house". Thatcherites also assumed that contracting-out would improve the quality of service provision, because of competition between private companies either to obtain these contracts, or to have a current contract renewed near its expiry. Finally, by appointing managers from the private sector to oversee specific services in the public sector, in order to instil a business ethos into them, and change the staff's working culture. For example, it is now quite common for some university vice-chancellors to have previously been senior managers of a major private company, rather than life-long academics. They are appointed to render the university more business-like in terms of attracting more customers (students), introducing more cost-effective, efficient, or flexible, working practices, and raising more revenue generally, by requiring academic staff to seek external research funding – "grant capture".

All of these measures and reforms were intended to change the ethos and practices of public services by compelling them to imitate or incorporate the supposedly more efficient and consumer-responsive practices of the private sector. The preferences of service users were to be prioritized over those of service providers and public sector professionals, and funding was to be increasingly linked to success either in attracting more customers or/and reaching performance targets imposed from above. These new funding mechanisms were partly intended to replicate the profit motive which drives the private sector, and thereby incentivize public sector workers to become more competitive (with comparable institutions), increase their productivity, and improve the quality of the service(s) they provided.

Managerialism

In tandem with marketization, Thatcherites also deemed it essential that professionals employed in education, healthcare, probation and social work were subjected to stronger and more direct modes of top-down management. This, of course, reflected the Thatcherite view that many public sector employees had cushy jobs-for-life followed by gold-plated pensions when they retired in their 50s, and therefore needed to be compelled to work much harder under the leadership and surveillance of strong managers. Consequently, Thatcherism heralded a fetishization of strong leadership throughout the public sector, and more rigorous modes of top-down governance, and these were continued under New Labour and all subsequent governments.

In education, for example, the emphasis on strong leadership yielded an adulation of heroic school headmasters/headmistresses and university vice-chancellors, supposedly with the drive, strategic leadership and vision to transform their institutions into excellent, even world-class, schools and universities (Wright 2001). Moreover, in accordance with the emphasis on individualism within neoliberalism, any success enjoyed by a school or university was variously attributed to the acumen or skills of the leaders, while downplaying the efforts, efficiency and professionalism of the teaching staff themselves, and thereby denying the extent to which organizational or sectoral achievements are largely derived from collective and collegial endeavour based on collaborative teamwork. This was yet another way in which the governance of public sector organizations imitated the private sector, because in the latter, corporate success is invariably credited to the business acumen and strategic leadership provided by the CEO, rather than the collective and combined efforts of customer-facing or shop-floor staff; whether it was a supermarket or a school, Thatcherism deemed success to derive from strong and effective leadership.

This shift to managerialism also meant that throughout the public sector since the 1980s, there has been a significant increase in the number – and authority – of managers and associated senior administrative staff, whose role is to render the institution or sector more business-like, cost-effective, efficient, productive and results-orientated. This hyper-managerialist regime has had profound consequences for the autonomy, discretion, expertise and professional judgement previously enjoyed and exercised by public sector staff. Increasingly, doctors, nurses, probation officers, social workers, teachers and university lecturers, have been subjected to a plethora of procedural requirements and regulatory frameworks dictating not just *what* they are expected to do, but *how* they perform their roles and tasks, and *which* outcomes are expected to be achieved or prioritized.

Furthermore, every activity must now be recorded and documented, and the correct boxes ticked, so that there is always a so-called evidence trail in case a complaint is subsequently lodged, or in readiness for the next external audit or inspection to evaluate how far the institution is fit for purpose, is providing a high-quality service, and/or providing value for money for taxpayers. Increasing amounts of staff time and energy are now devoted to box-ticking, data-entry, form-filling and report-writing, to prove not only that designated tasks have been completed and specified objectives achieved, but that these have been performed and attained in the prescribed manner: the bureaucratic tail now wags the professional dog. All under a neoliberal regime which purports to venerate individual freedom, and denounces red tape or political interference (see Garnett 2004; and Chapter 6).

Yet these robust administrative procedures do not automatically guarantee that a quality service has been provided; the correct boxes might be ticked, but what was received by, or delivered to, the client might have been barely satisfactory. One of the problems of evaluating public sector performance is that measurements are often quantitative, rather than qualitative, because it is usually easier to measure outputs in simple numerical terms than measure how well the tasks were performed. For example, if surgeon A performs 10 operations in a day while surgeon B performs 5 operations, it will be widely assumed that surgeon A is twice as efficient and hard-working than surgeon B. However, it might be that surgeon A rushes their operations, and thus fails to exercise sufficient care, to the extent that some of their patients are subsequently readmitted to hospital for further surgery or other remedial treatment, whereas supposedly less efficient surgeon B exercises great care and diligence in their operations, such that their patients make a full and long-lasting recovery.

Elsewhere, the police have increasingly complained that pressure to hit targets for arrests and convictions means that they feel compelled to focus on easier (but arguably less serious) offences, because more serious or complex crimes will take longer to investigate and gather evidence, and thereby result in fewer arrests and prosecutions, at least in the short term. Again, quantitative targets and simplistic measurements of efficiency are prioritized over qualitative criteria and more sophisticated modes of evaluation.

One other way in which public sector professionals have seen their expertise downgraded is by their exclusion from discussions with ministers and senior civil servants over policies pertaining to education, healthcare, policing, probation and social work. Prior to the Thatcher governments, there was generally a close and collaborative relationship between a minister, his/her department, and the relevant professional association(s) or trade union(s): political scientists termed these "policy communities" (Marsh & Rhodes 1992). For example, the education policy community had consisted of the secretary of state for education, senior officials in the Department of Education, leaders of the main teaching unions, and leaders of local education authorities.

Thatcherism naturally rejected this consensual and collaborative approach to policy-making in the public sector. Not only was this deemed redolent of the corporatist politics and trade union influence that Thatcherites firmly rejected, and a contributory factor in the postwar expansion of the state, via the public sector and its relentless lobbying for more resources, many ministers no longer considered it necessary to seek the advice or cooperation of public sector professionals. Instead, public sector compliance would be secured through the dual imposition of the market and managerial discipline. If public sector institutions and their workers refused or failed to implement or achieve what ministers stipulated, then sanctions were likely to be imposed, or their funding reduced, whereupon redundancies would almost certainly ensue. Alternatively, the institution or service might be contracted-out to the private sector.

Meanwhile, if individual staff members in the public sector refused or failed to perform as required, and thus did not achieve specified results, they were likely to "fail" their annual appraisals or be disciplined by management, and ultimately be dismissed from their jobs. Managerialism has thus seen a consensual and collaborative approach to public sector governance replaced by an often combative and sometimes confrontational style of management, which replicates the stance adopted by governments and ministers themselves.

Restoring law and order

Although Thatcherism extolled greater freedom and liberty in the economic sphere, and thus the objective of rolling back the state (although trade union reform entailed extensive state intervention, of course, precisely because the unions were viewed both as an obstacle to the smooth operation of the market, and to the exercise of managerial authority by employers), in sundry other policy spheres, the emphasis was very much on rolling the state forward to impose more authority and social discipline. This was particularly true in terms of tackling crime and other forms or anti-social or delinquent behaviour. As noted in the previous chapter, Thatcherism believed that since the 1960s, Britain had suffered from a surfeit of permissiveness, where liberty had morphed into licence for some individuals to behave selfishly or irresponsibly, without any regard for other people or their property. Thatcherism was therefore determined to restore law and order, and make Britain's streets safer for ordinary people to pursue their lawful and legitimate business, by increasing both the number of police officers and their powers to tackle crime, and other forms of disorder such as demonstrations or protests.

More generally, Thatcher and her ministerial colleagues would brook no criticism of the police or their conduct, insisting that the "thin blue line" against criminality and social breakdown must always be supported, and that law-abiding people had nothing to fear from the police. Anyone who criticized the conduct of the police, or accused them of targeting specific minorities, was invariably denounced as politically motivated, or of being on the side of criminality and disorder because they were, in effect, undermining the police. Similarly, if a protestor claimed to have been the victim of over-zealous policing, perhaps having been injured by a police truncheon, the Thatcherite response was likely to have been that they "must have been doing something" to have provoked the police response, or even that it "served them right" for protesting in the first place; they should either have stayed at home, been at work/college, or been looking for a job.

Meanwhile, courts and judges were empowered or encouraged to impose longer prison sentences on those found guilty of committing particular crimes. Pledging to get tough or crackdown on crime – perhaps while ostentatiously holding aloft a set of handcuffs – was always very popular with Conservative delegates at the party's annual conferences, whose only disappointment with the Thatcher governments with regard to penal policy was the failure to restore the death penalty for the most serious crimes (the House of Commons has consistently voted against restoration of capital punishment).

Cutting welfare provision

The welfare state was a key target for the Thatcher governments for economic *and* moral reasons, as noted in the previous chapter. Supposedly generous or easily-obtained welfare benefits were simultaneously criticized for being a major cause of high taxation and public expenditure, and for undermining the work ethic and individual self-reliance by creating a dependency culture. Thatcherites also strongly resented the extent to which the welfare state was intended to achieve the left's goal of creating greater equality by redistributing wealth from the rich via punitive taxes, to the poor through allegedly generous social security benefits. Thatcher and many of her closest colleagues were also convinced that welfarism was undermining the traditional family (a married heterosexual couple) by making it too easy or financially attractive for young women to become single parents, not only through divorce, but by eschewing marriage altogether.

The Thatcherite war on welfare was multifaceted, the main changes and curbs were as follows:

- De-index-linking social security increases, so that benefits were no longer raised in tandem with increases in average earnings, but instead increased in tandem with the rate of inflation. As the latter was often slightly lower than the increase in earnings, this ensured savings for the Treasury, while also ensuring that fewer people would be better-off receiving benefits instead of working.
- The abolition of the earnings-related supplement, whereby new claimants initially received a top-up payment linked to their previous wage or salary, intended to help them adjust to their suddenly changed economic status and lower income overall.
- The unemployed were subjected to an increasingly rigorous surveillance regime, whereby they were regularly summoned for interview by social security staff, who sought evidence that the claimant was actively seeking work. Failure to provide such evidence was likely to result in benefits being cut as punishment.
- The former system of grants paid to social security claimants who needed to replace essential household items such as a bed or cooker was replaced by a social fund. This was a loan which would then be repaid out of the claimant's benefits. This yielded further savings for the Treasury, and was intended to instil financial responsibility in claimants, although in practice, it often caused greater financial hardship, because after their loan repayment was deducted from their social security benefit, they had even less money to spend on food, clothes and domestic fuel bills.
- Child Benefit rates were frozen in some years, so that parents received no increase.
- Social security benefits became taxable. This did not mean that claimants had income tax deducted from their weekly benefits, but that when they started work, the amount of social security they had received in that financial year would be considered when calculating their tax allowance: namely, how much they could earn before they started paying income tax.

In tandem with these reforms and restrictions, Thatcherism adopted a disparaging discourse when referring to some welfare claimants, reflecting the right's deeply ingrained assumption that many of the unemployed were simply lazy and work-shy, or that many unmarried mothers were sexually promiscuous, and were enabled by the allegedly easy availability of supposedly lucrative social security benefits. Even today, in spite of repeated curbs on eligibility to receive social security benefits, the strict conditions which have to be met by claimants, and the sundry reports about the financial hardship and poverty endured by many welfare recipients, Conservatives (and much of the media and the public) still insist that benefits are too high, too easily attained, and that being unemployed or a single parent is an attractive and rewarding life-style choice encouraged or facilitated by the supposedly over-generous welfare state (Dorey 2010b).

Promoting "family values"

Although it proved politically impossible to impose or enforce via legislation, Thatcherism made clear its strong preference for families that comprised a heterosexual married couple, and children born and raised within marriage. It was also made clear that, ideally, this family should enshrine a clear sexual division of labour, whereby the husband was the sole or main wage/salary earner (breadwinner), while the wife was expected to accept that her primary roles were cooking, cleaning, looking after the children, and providing her husband with regular sex (not until the early 1990s did marital rape become a criminal offence). The Thatcherite vision of the family was thus clearly a patriarchal one, in which men, as husbands, were economically dominant and their sexual desires paramount.

Consequently, Thatcherites disapproved of other family forms and sexual relationships, and often viewed them as symptomatic of Britain's moral decline; since the 1960s, there had apparently been too much permissiveness and promiscuity – although, of course, the pejorative term "promiscuous" was (and still is) only applied to women who enjoyed casual, non-monogamous or polyamorous sexual encounters, whereas men who have multiple sexual partners or frequent one-night stands are still widely revered as "studs", while women with a healthy sexual appetite who do likewise are still routinely "slut-shamed" or misogynistically labelled "nymphomaniacs".

The Thatcherite veneration of the heterosexual family meant that there was strong disapproval of same-sex relationships. Indeed, homophobia on the right was reinforced by the AIDS epidemic of the latter half of the 1980s, which was referred to by some tabloids as the "Gay Plague" because of the extent to which the often fatal (at that time) sexually transmitted disease – which killed Queen singer Freddie Mercury – affected gay men. There were even claims by some homophobes that AIDS was God's wrath against gay men, a vengeful punishment of people accused of engaging in allegedly deviant sexual practices and depraved lifestyles.

Not surprisingly, AIDS proved problematic for the Thatcher governments, because even when scientific evidence illustrated that the epidemic was increasingly affecting heterosexuals, rather than solely LGBT communities, there was disagreement about the extent to which ministers should promote a "safe sex" campaign via advocacy of using condoms, rather than highlight the need for sexual abstinence and chastity, in accordance with traditional morality and Victorian values. The social services secretary at the time, Norman Fowler, was adamant that the AIDS epidemic was sufficiently serious and life-threatening to require an urgent public health campaign, via leaflets delivered to homes, and full-page adverts in newspapers, on television, in cinemas, and on public billboards, graphically explaining how the virus was spread, and how it could be curbed via "safe sex". The graphic content was deemed necessary to alert the public to the seriousness of the pandemic, and to challenge the complacency of those citizens who assumed that because they were not gay, AIDS could not affect them.

Initially, Thatcher was horrified by the explicit content and details in the proposed adverts, and in one of her hand-written comments on correspondence submitted to her, asked "Do we have to do the section on Risky sex?" Her initial preference was to confine the public health campaign against AIDS to leaflets or posters in doctors' surgeries and public toilets, rather than "place advertisements in newspapers which every young person could read and learn of practices they never knew about", and which might encourage them to ask their parents embarrassing questions. Thatcher deemed a comprehensive and explicit advertising campaign promoting "safe sex" as unnecessary, particularly as most people "would never be in danger from AIDS" (NA 1986c). However, Thatcher was eventually persuaded by Fowler, one of her SPADs, David Willetts, and the chief medical officer, that a graphic public health campaign, coupled with promotion of "safe sex" via condom use, were vital due to the scale of the pandemic, and the (then) lack of a cure (Fowler 1991: ch. 13; NA 1986c).

A clear manifestation of the Thatcherite disapproval of same-sex relationships was Section 28 of the 1988 Local Government Act, which decreed that in school sex education lessons, teachers must not "promote" homosexuality by depicting same-sex relationships as acceptable or in any way normal (Baker 2022; Wakefield & Kelleher 2021). Thatcher herself had complained at the 1987 Conservative Party conference that: "Children who need to be taught to respect traditional moral values are being taught that they have an inalienable right to be gay … those children are being cheated of a sound start in life" (TF 1987). At that time, 75 per cent of British people believed that same-sex relations were "always or mostly wrong" (Sommerlad 2018).

Also subject to Thatcherite disapproval, as noted earlier, were single parents, especially unmarried mothers who were reliant on welfare payments in the absence of a (breadwinner) husband or long-term boyfriend. Thatcher herself complained that aspects of the welfare state provided "positive incentives to irresponsible conduct. Young girls were tempted to become pregnant because that brought them a council flat and an income from the state" (Thatcher 1993: 629). Similarly, Nicholas Ridley condemned a system which ensured that "without husband, without job, and without effort, young girls could house, clothe and feed themselves at the taxpayers' expense, provided they had children … free-riders on the system, directly exploiting the dependency culture". The apparent benevolence of the welfare state, Ridley complained, meant that: "It became a way of living for some [young women] to have one or more children by unknown men, in order to qualify for a council house" (Ridley 1991: 91; see also Tebbit 1991: 97).

Increasing Euroscepticism

During her premiership, Thatcher became increasingly Eurosceptic, to the extent that her hostility to the European Community (EC - it did not become the European Union until the 1993 Maastricht Treaty) eventually contributed to her downfall in November 1990. Thatcher had campaigned for the UK to remain in the EC in the 1975 referendum, but during her premiership, the crystallization and solidification of her economically neoliberal, socially authoritarian and English nationalist views made her increasingly critical of the EC. Her growing Euroscepticism was also reinforced by parallel developments emanating from the EC itself, which also fuelled anti-European attitudes among other MPs on the right of the Conservative Party (Dorey 2017).

Thatcher's Euroscepticism was prompted by three particular developments or issues. The first concerned Britain's budgetary contributions to the EC during the early 1980s, and how the EC budget was subsequently spent. The two main sources of the EC's budget were 1 per cent of each member state's annual VAT (or equivalent) revenues, and tariffs charged on a country's imports from outside the EC. The first of these sources was a major problem for the Thatcher governments, because in his very first Budget, just weeks after the May 1979 election victory, Geoffrey Howe had (as noted above) almost doubled VAT from 8 to 15 per cent, to offset the slashing of income tax for the better-off. Consequently, 1 per cent of the Treasury's annual VAT receipts was much more, in cash terms, than the corresponding amount contributed by other EC member states.

The Thatcher government's objection to how much Britain was contributing was compounded by the other main source of the EC's income, namely contributions linked to each member state's imports from beyond the EC itself. This was a highly salient issue for Britain due to the continued trading links with, and thus imports (especially dairy produce and meat) from, the Commonwealth, because these added to Britain's budgetary contributions to the EC; other member states did not have comparable trading links with non-EC countries, and so were not obliged to make similar payments on non-EC imports. This naturally fuelled Thatcher's antipathy to the EC, and her complaint that Britain was contributing far more than other member states (George 1998: 132; Howe 1994: ch. 27; Renwick 2013: ch. 7; Wall 2008: ch. 2).

However, it was not only the amount that Britain was contributing to the EC's budget due to these two sources, but also the fact that about 66 per cent of this budget was then spent via the Common Agricultural Policy (CAP). Yet Britain was not an agricultural nation with a large farming industry, and therefore derived little financial benefit from the CAP (George 1998: 133). Indeed, there was an irony in that Britain's contributions to the EC's budget were boosted by the country's agricultural imports from the Commonwealth, whereupon two-thirds of this budget were subsequently disbursed to the agricultural sectors and farmers in other EC member states. This scenario fuelled a five-year dispute with the EC, as Thatcher demanded "our money back". Eventually, at an EC summit in Fontainebleau in June 1984, an agreement was reached whereby Britain was awarded a substantial annual rebate (for details, see George 1998: ch. 5; Young 2000: 130–37).

Two years later, the Single European Act (SEA) heralded the move towards a single European market, entailing the removal of border controls and customs duties on intra-EC trade, and facilitating the free movement of goods, capital, and labour (workers) between member states. The SEA was wholly commensurate with Thatcherism's enthusiastic commitment to economic liberalism and free trade. As Nicholas Ridley declared, "[we] were wholeheartedly in favour of the provisions

Opposition leader Margaret Thatcher shows her European colours in Parliament Square as she links up with the young pro-market campaigners on the day before polling for the Common Market referendum, 4 June 1975 (courtesy of PA Images/ Alamy Stock Photo).

relating to the Single Market ... An open market in Europe was what we had always wanted" (Ridley 1991: 143).

However, the SEA also entailed reform of EC decision-taking, by extending the range of issues and policies which would be determined by qualified majority voting (QMV), rather than by unanimity whereby *all* member states had to agree to a proposal before it could be officially adopted. The switch to QMV clearly reduced the scope for individual member states and their governments to veto proposals that they judged to be inimical to their economic or political interests, and this, in effect, further impinged upon Britain's (parliamentary) sovereignty. At the time, however, "the importance which Thatcherites attached to the promotion of the single market" was such that the non-economic implications of the SEA were discretely disregarded (Letwin 1992: 284).

Also, while innocuous at that time, the free movement of labour became a toxic issue three decades later, when migrant workers from Poland and Romania (which joined the EU in 2004 and 2007 respectively) were often blamed for "taking British workers' jobs" or driving down wages. This resentment was often most prominent in deindustrialized or so-called "left-behind" towns in parts of northern England and the East Midlands, where EU migrants were readily blamed for causing unemployment, low wages, burdening already over-stretched public services, and exacerbating shortages of housing, in an era of austerity. Indeed, for many Leave voters in the 2016 EU referendum, halting and reversing immigration from Europe was their prime objective or motive for supporting Brexit.

The third development, which fuelled Thatcherism's growing Euroscepticism, was the emergence, in the late 1980s, of a "social Europe" agenda, whereby the transition to a single market and free trade would be matched by a corresponding increase in employment protection and rights for workers whose conditions or security of employment were likely to be jeopardized by greater economic liberalization, competition and deregulation. Thatcher was naturally wholly in favour of extending economic freedom, but implacably opposed to strengthening employment protection and workers' rights vis-à-vis their employers, measures which she viewed both as socialist, and a source of trade union power, as well as wholly incompatible with the neoliberal promotion of labour market flexibility and management's right to manage. This antipathy was evident in her notorious 1988 Bruges speech, when she attacked "those who see European unity as a vehicle for spreading socialism" and warned that: "We haven't worked all these years to free Britain from paralysis of socialism only to see it creep through the back door of central control and bureaucracy in Brussels" (TF 1988a).

By the end of her premiership, therefore, Thatcher had become deeply concerned at the direction in which the EC was seemingly being steered: "I had witnessed a profound shift in how European policy was conducted – and therefore in the kind of Europe that was taking shape. A Franco-German bloc with its own agenda had re-emerged to set the direction of the Community". This development, she claimed, was being facilitated both by the European Commission, "which had always had a yen for centralised power", and Britain's own Foreign Office which "was almost imperceptibly moving to compromise" with the key policy actors shaping the future of the EC (Thatcher 1993: 558–9; see also Ridley 1990: 8–9).

Thatcher's increasing Euroscepticism was also a consequence of her clear prioritization of the purported special relationship with the United States during the 1980s, which she considered to be much more important, reliable and valuable than closer ties with Britain's West European neighbours. The Anglo-American alliance was strengthened by two developments during the decade. First, the election of Ronald Reagan as US president, who served from 1981 to 1989, and was an ideological kindred spirit to Thatcher. Both leaders were economic neoliberals, social conservatives with authoritarian tendencies, and both were vehemently anti-socialist; indeed they discerned little difference between socialism and communism, viewing them as two sides of the same coin.

The second development, which led Thatcher to prioritize Anglo-American relations over closer ties with the EC, was an intensification of the Cold War during the early to mid-1980s, and an increasingly hostile stance by Thatcher and Reagan towards the Soviet Union. Not only did they routinely denounce its dictatorial political system and lack of human rights or civil liberties, they also insisted that it was an aggressive and expansionist regime, which posed a serious threat to the West and the free world. This was deemed to necessitate a stronger defence policy and enhanced military capability, including upgraded nuclear weaponry, to deter an attack or invasion emanating from Moscow.

Yet brutal and barbaric though the Soviet regime certainly was, Thatcher and Reagan were not averse to citing the threat of communism

Prime Minister Margaret Thatcher makes a statement following her meeting with President Reagan outside the White House, 20 February 1985 (courtesy of dpa picture alliance/Alamy Stock Photo).

to justify illiberal or repressive measures of their own, with left-wing activists sometimes vetted or placed under surveillance by the security services, or critics of Thatcherism accused of being unpatriotic or even "Soviet sympathizers"; for example, during the 1980s, members and supporters of the Campaign for Nuclear Disarmament (CND) were variously accused of being Soviet "stooges" or funded by the KGB, on the basis that the only regime which would benefit from Britain renouncing its nuclear weapons would be the Soviet Union. Thatcher and Reagan also supported, or pretended not to see, the imprisonment, torture and other flagrant human rights abuses routinely practiced by authoritarian regimes and right-wing military juntas in Central and South America, on the grounds that these regimes were resisting communism – by treating critics and political opponents in exactly the same brutal way that the Soviet Union treated its dissidents and internal enemies.

A new style of policy-making

As alluded to above, the Thatcher governments largely excluded the trade unions and professional associations from the policy-making process; the corridors of power were closed to them. This was a deliberate and ideologically-driven departure from the previous consultative or neo-corporatist style of policy-making which had mostly prevailed since 1945, both at macro-level, via the NEDC, and at the sectoral or meso-level, such as education and health. During this pre-Thatcher era of British political history, the emphasis had been on consensus, both in terms of broad agreement between the senior politicians in the Conservative and Labour Parties over many policies and governmental objectives, and in the extent to which key organized interests and professional bodies, such as the BMA, had routinely been involved in policy development in their sphere, thereby playing a major role in shaping the policies.

Indeed, some political scientists argued that before Thatcher's premiership, Britain had been characterized by a clear British policy style, entailing regular and routinized elite-level bargaining and negotiation between ministers, senior civil servants, and the leaders of key organized interests or professional associations (Jordan & Richardson 1982). It had usually been generally accepted by ministers that the relevant organized interests or sectoral/professional associations ought to be closely consulted over policies in their field, both as a matter of principle or good will, and because of the practical advice and expertise they could offer ministers and senior civil servants in the formulation and implementation of policies. This established a form of neo-corporatism or social partnership which aimed to secure the consent of the governed, and which was assumed to reflect the norms and values of a liberal democratic polity; policies based on regular discussion and institutionalized dialogue with the relevant representative bodies, rather than arbitrarily imposed by ministerial decree or diktat, as they would be in an authoritarian or Soviet-style regime.

Unsurprisingly, just as Thatcherism rejected the policies associated with the post-1945 consensus, so too did Thatcherites eschew the consensual mode of policy-making which had characterized this era. They believed that policies should be determined by a democratically-elected government whose political authority derived from those who had voted it into power; this reflected the executive-orientated Westminster model of British government (Judge 2005: 24–6; Rhodes 1997: 5–7; Smith 1999: 9–11). Moreover, governments should have the autonomy to make decisions and adopt policies that they judged to be in the national interest and/or promoted wealth-creating entrepreneurship and private-sector business activity. From this perspective, policy-making in Britain had hitherto granted too much power to unelected, unaccountable and unrepresentative sectional or professional interests, who had been permitted – due to the search for consensus – to limit policy options, and thus constrain what decisions government and ministers could take. Furthermore, Thatcherites believed that this mode of policy-making often meant that tough or unpopular, but ultimately economically necessary, decisions and radical policies were avoided or abandoned, because they would not enjoy the agreement of the supposedly self-serving and selfish organized interests involved.

Consequently, Thatcher's self-proclaimed conviction politics meant that policies were increasingly derived from ideological assumptions and objectives, reflecting what Thatcherites judged necessary to tackle economic, industrial and social problems, and inter alia secure a paradigm shift in British politics and political economy. In pursuing this new approach, Thatcherites did not care how much condemnation and hostility they attracted from organized interests and professional associations who suddenly found themselves excluded from the corridors of power. On the contrary, Thatcher, and her closest ministers and special advisers, seemed to relish goading (or what today might be termed "trolling") prominent individuals – even in her own party – and institutions who criticized the new policies and/or her style of leadership. Policies, which had hitherto been based on maximum agreement and acceptability, were now often implemented in an adversarial and authoritarian manner. Ministerial diktats replaced meaningful dialogue, and critics either ignored or removed.

4

Thatcher's management and domination of the parliamentary Conservative Party

Throughout her premiership, Margaret Thatcher led a party in which, according to Philip Norton (1990), only 19 per cent of Conservative MPs and ministers fully shared and supported her political views and vision, yet she and her eponymous ideology enjoyed considerable dominance, both intellectually and in terms of policy objectives (the parliamentary rejection of the 1986 Shops Bill to legalize Sunday trading was Thatcher's only parliamentary defeat in the 1980s). Seven factors underpinned this dominance, and thereby the entrenchment of Thatcherism until it had established intellectual hegemony and a path-dependency, namely: (1) her allocation of cabinet posts and ministerial portfolios; (2) her combative style in chairing cabinet meetings, ministerial committees or conducting bilateral meetings with individual ministers to determine policy; (3) the recruitment of ideologically-aligned special advisers (SPADS) to the Downing Street Policy Unit and, sometimes, elsewhere in Whitehall; (4) the successful manner in which she responded to specific major events or crises which might have undermined other prime ministers; (5) the loyalty of most Conservative MPs whose support was extensively based on her electoral success rather than wholehearted or fervent ideological agreement; (6) the extent to which her critics and opponents in the parliamentary Conservative Party both underestimated her sheer determination and tenacity, and were unable to articulate a coherent or convincing alternative; and (7) the weakness of the non-Conservative opposition generally, not only ideologically and in terms of (lack of) leadership credibility, but due also to the vicissitudes of Britain's simple plurality or first-past-the-post electoral system which fragments, and thus effectively weakens the impact of, public support enjoyed by the other political parties among British voters.

Thatcher's allocation of cabinet posts and ministerial portfolios

It has become common wisdom that during her premiership, Thatcher appointed a cabinet of "Yes Men", a perspective ostensibly lent credence by the well-publicized dismissals of prominent critics, usually from the left or One Nation wing of the parliamentary Conservative Party, whose more general ideological weakness is discussed below. During her first term (1979–83), Thatcher dismissed non-believers such as Mark Carlisle, Ian Gilmour, Lord (Christopher) Soames and Norman St John Stevas, while the Conservatives' emphatic victory in the 1983 election heralded the sacking of Francis Pym. Yet rather than completely exclude, or conduct wholesale purges of, her critics to craft a wholly Thatcherite cabinet, Thatcher was generally shrewder in her ministerial appointments, allocating what she deemed to be the most important posts and portfolios, mainly those concerned with economic and industrial affairs, to those colleagues who she trusted to be "one of us": ministers who shared her ideological outlook and objectives (Shepherd 1991: 181).

What this meant, in practice, was that fellow neoliberals were usually allocated to the key economic ministries; for example, Geoffrey Howe, and then Nigel Lawson, served as chancellors from 1979 to 1989, with political responsibility for controlling public spending and cutting direct taxes, whereas Keith Joseph, Cecil Parkinson, Nicholas Ridley, Norman Tebbit, and Lord (David) Young all served stints at the Department of Trade and Industry, from where privatization and deregulation were actively pursued. Another key economic ministry, from a Thatcherite perspective, was the Department of Employment, which oversaw the programme of trade union reform and deregulation of the labour market, and inter alia, the increasing transfer of power from shopfloor to company boardroom, and from workers to employers. After the wholly expected removal of the ultra-conciliatory James Prior in the September 1981 cabinet reshuffle, Thatcherites such as Tebbit and Lord (David) Young variously served as employment secretaries, the former especially having acquired a reputation as a "union basher", even though he sometimes proceeded a little more cautiously than his supporters wanted in legislating to curb the power of the unions (Tebbit 1988: 197–8).

Thatcher recognized that she could not fill her cabinet solely with her ideological acolytes, but that a range of views from within the

Conservative Party needed to be included, both in order to maintain some public semblance of unity, and to encourage non-Thatcherites on the party's backbenches to believe that their voice and views were being heard in the cabinet. However, there was also a constitutional consideration, namely that of collective ministerial responsibility, meaning that non-Thatcherite ministers would be required publicly to defend specific policies with which they might privately disagree. As the former US president, Lyndon B. Johnson, pithily put it, "better to have your enemies inside the tent pissing out, than outside the tent pissing in". Certainly, Prior noted that the very first (1979–81) Thatcher cabinet was probably the most divided cabinet ever, due to the divisions between the One Nation Tory wets and Thatcherite dries: "There was a deep division on economic and social policy" (Prior 1986: 134; see also TF 1981a).

Some cabinet ministers were appointed, not for their ideological purity or because Thatcher viewed them as "one of us", but because they were judged either to be sufficiently loyal and competent to enact policies within their departmental remit, such as Leon Brittan at the Home Office (1983–85), and Norman Fowler at the Department of Health

Thatcher's new cabinet, 7 July 1983 (courtesy of PA Images/Alamy Stock Photo)

(1981-87), or because they were judged by Thatcher to be effective communicators, such as William Whitelaw and Peter Walker. It was reasoned that if respected non-Thatcherite ministers such as Whitelaw and Walker were presented to the media to defend and explain particular policies, they would be more likely to convince ordinary British people of the efficacy or necessity of the policies. Certainly, Walker was deemed vital to explaining, in a calm but authoritative manner, the Thatcher government's stance during the bitter 1984-85 miners' strike, and thereby ensuring that ministers retained public support in resolutely standing firm against Arthur Scargill and the NUM (See, e.g., TF 1984b; Walker 1991: 166).

Meanwhile, ministers who were not deemed "one of us" were often allocated to departments or ministerial portfolios that Thatcher viewed as having a low profile or status, and thus peripheral to her core economic priorities. For example, upon becoming prime minister, she appointed Michael Heseltine secretary of state for the environment, which, in the 1980s, was not about the environment in terms of climate change, but primarily about matters pertaining to building regulations, local government and town planning – although its profile was subsequently raised by the Thatcherite policy of selling council houses to their tenants. Another non-Thatcherite, Nicholas Edwards, was appointed to the post of secretary of state for Wales (clearly not a role that Thatcher viewed as central to her primary objectives and policy goals), whilst James Prior's transfer to the Northern Ireland Office, in the autumn 1981 cabinet reshuffle, was certainly not a reward or promotion after he had repeatedly infuriated Thatcher and her ideological allies with his softly-softly approach to trade union reform.

One other tactic Thatcher occasionally deployed when appointing cabinet ministers who she knew were *not* ideologically aligned with her was to appoint at least one of their junior ministers, namely someone who she trusted. For example, when she appointed Prior as employment secretary in 1979, she also insisted that Sir Patrick Mayhew served as one of his junior ministers, informing Prior that "I'm determined to have *someone* with backbone in your Department", although Prior subsequently cultivated a constructive working relationship with Mayhew (Prior 1986: 114, emphasis in original).

Her combative style in conducting government business

There are three aspects of Thatcher's leadership style and interactions with ministers to consider under this heading. The first concerns the manner in which she reportedly chaired cabinet meetings, the second highlights the way in which she often preferred to conduct political business through one-to-one meetings with ministers, albeit with Thatcher herself sometimes accompanied by a few of her own officials or SPADs, and the third relates to the thoroughness, and sometimes acerbic manner, in which she read and annotated papers and policy proposals submitted to her by ministerial colleagues, sometimes returning them with excoriating comments and criticisms.

The chairing of cabinet meetings

Just a few weeks before the 1979 general election, Thatcher had warned that if she became prime minister, "I could not waste time having any internal arguments ... it must be a cabinet that works on something much more than pragmatism or consensus. It must be a conviction government" (Thatcher 1979). This reflected a combination of Thatcher's ideological vision and her personality, for she "believed absolutely in her own integrity and habitually disparaged the motives of those who disagreed with her ... Margaret's temperament was ... combative", reflecting and reinforcing the extent to which "politically and socially, she saw the world in black and white, and divided people, institutions and countries into ... 'us' to be encouraged and rewarded, 'them' to be defeated and destroyed" (Campbell 2000: 31).

This assertion foretold Thatcher's style when chairing the Thursday morning meetings of the cabinet, when she would sometimes state her own view or stance on a specific issue or policy proposal, and then rhetorically enquire if any of her colleagues disagreed; few dared to demur (Shepherd 191: 202). Having served during both the Thatcher and the Major premierships, Chris Patten wryly recalled that in the latter: "We got the summing up at the end of cabinet, rather than the beginning" (quoted in Hogg & Hill 1995: 13).

Not only did this style of chairing the cabinet (and cabinet committees, see below) deter or minimize ministerial discussions on some policy issues, it also reduced the length of such meetings, which is doubtless what Thatcher intended. The eminent political historian Lord (Peter) Hennessy reports an occasion when a senior minister entered the House of Commons tea-room late one Thursday morning. Upon seeing him, a Conservative MP asked why he was not in cabinet (which usually met at 10 am), to which the minister replied: "Cabinet? Oh, we don't have those anymore. We have a lecture by Madam", adding that in the absence of collective discussions: "Half the decisions I read about in the newspapers" (Hennessy 1986: 99).

On other occasions, Thatcher would subject the relevant minister to rigorous questioning when they outlined their own position or policy proposal, virtually cross-examining them in the presence of their cabinet colleagues. This reflected both Thatcher's own combative personal style, and her background as a barrister, although she and her closest acolytes naturally defended this approach as a means of testing the robustness of a policy proposal, and/or the validity of the evidence or prognosis on which it was based; the onus was on the minister to defend their position or perspective, and persuade Thatcher of the virtues and veracity of the solution or legislation that they were advocating.

This adversarial style of conducting cabinet business naturally caused anxiety and apprehension in some ministers, particularly those who recognized that they were not considered to be "one of us", and who were therefore particularly vulnerable to incurring Thatcher's displeasure, and possibly being humiliated in front of their ministerial colleagues. According to Prior, she "not only starts with a spirit of confrontation but continues with it right through the argument" (Prior 1986: 138). As another minister in the 1979–83 cabinet subsequently reflected, "I don't regard high-pitched argument as the best means of reaching decisions … I don't think one should argue right from the start" (David Howell, quoted in Hennessy 1986: 97).

One of Thatcher's private secretaries has acknowledged her "hectoring behaviour" towards some ministers (Slocock 2018: 158). Similarly, her chief press secretary recalls that "she could be very direct, not to say tactless, with ministers to their faces" (Ingham 1991: 319; see also Waddington 2012: 225). It has even been claimed that a few ministers were "actually physically sick" before attending a cabinet meeting when they expected their position paper or policy proposal to be eviscerated by Thatcher (Hennessy 2001: 401).

The emollient (1979–81) employment secretary, James Prior, was naturally a prime target of Thatcher's impatience and irascibility in cabinet when he urged caution in pursuing trade union reform, and only proposed the bare minimum of legislation to regulate their activities. Indeed, after her very first cabinet, Lord (Nicholas) Soames sought to console Prior by claiming that "I wouldn't even treat my gamekeeper like that" (BBC1 1993). Another non-Thatcherite cabinet minister recalled "I learnt quickly that it was all too easy to find one's arguments cut off in midstream by prime ministerial interruption, to have the case one wished to deploy hijacked by premature conclusions, and often hectoring interventions" (Heseltine 2000: 232).

Yet even being much more ideologically aligned with Thatcher, especially on economic issues, did not always result in more courteous treatment, as Geoffrey Howe discovered. As foreign secretary from 1983 to 1989, his penchant for diplomacy and dialogue, and his increasingly pro-European views, naturally irked Thatcher, but her growing impatience with Howe was reinforced by his somewhat ponderous – some would say soporific – style of speaking, which sometimes tested the limits of her patience. As Nigel Lawson observed, she treated Howe "as a cross between a doormat and a punchbag" (quoted on BBC1 1993).

Eventually, one of her senior SPADS and ideological acolytes, John Hoskyns (TF 1981) became so appalled at her rude treatment of sundry ministerial colleagues that he sent Thatcher a memo admonishing her conduct: "You bully your weaker colleagues. You criticise your colleagues in front of each other, and in front of their officials. They can't answer back without appearing disrespectful … You abuse that situation. You give little praise or credit, and you are too ready to blame others when things go wrong". Hoskyns ceased to be one of Thatcher's advisers a few months later.

Thatcher's tendency to deter discussions, or interrupt ministers while they were speaking, was also a feature of some of the cabinet committees which she chaired, these being forums in which a few relevant (in policy terms) or carefully chosen ministers met to discuss an issue or policy in more detail than could be achieved in full cabinet, notwithstanding Thatcher's own antipathy to discussion and debate in this arena. Her brusqueness and impatience with Howe in the full cabinet was replicated in some cabinet committees. For example, as foreign secretary from 1983 to 1989, he had favoured establishing diplomatic relations with the newly elected government in Argentina, which had replaced the military junta that had invaded the Falkland Islands in March 1982 (see below). For Howe, this would necessitate reaching a diplomatic solution over the future governance of the Falklands, such as some mode of shared sovereignty between Britain and Argentina, or a leaseback scheme – options which had been mooted long before the Argentine invasion.

Thatcher, however, was implacably opposed to any such surrender or sharing of sovereignty, which she also deemed a betrayal of the Falkland Islanders who, ultimately, were British citizens. Consequently, when, in early 1984, Howe presented a paper to the cabinet committee on overseas and defence policy, in which he was intending to suggest establishing closer ties with Argentina in lieu of exploring options for the future governance of the Falklands, Thatcher interjected after just a few minutes, to declare "I know what you're going to recommend, Geoffrey, and the answer is No!" (Hennessy 1986: 99; see also Biffen 2013: 382). On another occasion, she berated Howe by declaring that: "Your paper is twaddle, complete and utter twaddle. I don't know how you have the nerve to submit it" (quoted in Aitken 2013: 562).

Howe also endured Thatcher's invective in cabinet committee meetings to discuss policy towards the European (Economic) Community, when his natural emollience and inclination towards diplomacy clashed with her suspicion that the Foreign and Commonwealth Office (FCO) was insufficiently resolute or robust in defending Britain's interest in international affairs. This scepticism has been shared by much of the Conservative right, as symbolized by Norman Tebbit's barbed quip that "the Ministry of Agriculture looks after the interests of farmers, and the Foreign Office looks after the interests of foreigners" (quoted in Jenkins 1989: 285). On one occasion, Thatcher "didn't just give Geoffrey a hand-bagging. He got a massive sand-bagging. She was just utterly and impossibly rude to him" (Bill Cash MP, quoted in Aitken 2013: 562).

Thatcher's penchant for conducting government business via bilaterals

Given her disdain for the type of collective discussion and decision-taking symbolized by the cabinet, it was not surprising that Thatcher evinced a marked preference for much smaller and more focused or ad hoc forums for reaching decisions and agreeing on policies, which meant that even cabinet committees were often bypassed. This lent itself to a penchant for bilaterals, entailing a face-to-face meeting with a minister, sometimes accompanied by her senior officials and/or SPADs (Hennessy 2001: 424; Kavanagh & Seldon 2000: 171; Lawson & Armstrong 1994: 443).

From Thatcher's perspective, such meetings were a much more effective use of her time due to the specificity of the issue or subject on the agenda, and the very limited number of participants, both of which greatly expedited the conduct of business and determination of policies. Conversely, however, they were often unnerving for the minister involved, particularly if they had a different perspective or policy preference to Thatcher. True, they would be spared potential humiliation in front of their cabinet colleagues, but they were instead faced by Thatcher (and her entourage) directly, and on her territory, namely a room in 10 Downing Street or her office in the House of Commons.

Her written responses to ministers' and civil servants' correspondence

An overlooked example of Thatcher's legendary brusqueness when dealing with ministers who incurred her annoyance, usually for the temerity of holding different political views or policy preferences, was the way she would annotate the letters and policy proposals they submitted to her for advice or approval. This aspect of her impatience with supposedly recalcitrant ministers has been uncovered by the voluminous correspondence accessible – open access – via the Thatcher Foundation's superb website; it is a veritable gold-mine for political historians of Thatcherism (https://www.margaretthatcher.org). Just five brief examples will suffice to provide a flavour of her curt responses to ministers whose written submissions provoked her ire.

Not surprisingly, James Prior was a key victim of Thatcher's written wrath, due to his correspondence and policy proposals urging caution in tackling the trade unions. On one paper he sent to Thatcher outlining his proposals for consulting with the TUC in advance of legislation, she had written, in the margin, that sending it on a Friday night in lieu of a press conference on Monday "just isn't good enough", and emphasizing, with regard to Prior's apparent sympathy with some of the TUC's arguments and objections, that "I am very unhappy about it", adding that it is "not our view" (NA 1979a). Another victim of Thatcher's acerbic hand-written comments was her first foreign secretary, Lord Carrington. In one of his early memos to her, about Britain's (controversial) contributions to the EC Budget, a clearly irked Thatcher complained that: "This is jabberwocky to me. What is it supposed to mean?" (NA 1979b).

Again, ideological affinity did not spare Geoffrey Howe from Thatcher's impatience, as expressed via her curt hand-written annotations. Within four weeks of the Conservatives' 1979 election victory, proposals submitted by Howe on how the new government should deal with pay in the public sector were brusquely dismissed by Thatcher with the hand-written comment that: "This is a very poor paper, and we can only charitably assume that the Treasury is otherwise occupied at the present" (NA 1979c). A subsequent paper on public-sector pay also received short shrift from Thatcher, who bluntly informed Howe, via her hand-written comments, that: "This is not in suitable format for cabinet discussion. Send it back to the Treasury and tell them to redraft it in accordance with standard [word illegible]". Thatcher added that: "We are getting far too many 'woolly' papers from the Treasury" (NA 1979d).

One other example of Thatcher's acerbic hand-written annotations occurred six years after the Falklands War, when Geoffrey Howe (him again!), now as foreign secretary, suggested a courtesy meeting with his Argentine counterpart at a United Nations summit in New York. Howe envisaged that this might precipitate a gradual normalization of diplomatic relations between the two countries, given that General Galtieri had long since ceased to be leader of Argentina. Thatcher, however, remained aghast at such a suggestion, claiming, via scribbled comments in the correspondence, that "this rather sticks in my gullet", and that "I utterly recoil from this" (NA 1988).

The deployment of ideologically aligned special advisers (SPADS)

Thatcher's ideological stance and combative style of leadership were reinforced by her appointment of like-minded SPADs to the 10 Downing

Street Policy Unit (on the role of this unit during the Thatcher premiership, see Willetts 1987). While the appointment of policy advisers was not in itself new or novel – they had been a notable feature of Harold Wilson's 1964–70 Labour premiership, particularly with regard to economic affairs – Thatcher made considerable use of such staff, both as a source of new or radical ideas with which to challenge established orthodoxies and Whitehall conservatism, and to provide her with intellectual reinforcement for policy preferences that she knew would not be fully shared by some of her ministerial colleagues (Hennessy 2001: 424; Yong & Hazell 2014: 23–4). Among those SPADs appointed by Thatcher, and who fully shared her ideological vision, were Brian Griffiths, John Hoskyns, Ferdinand Mount, John Redwood, Norman Strauss and Alan Walters.

Indeed, Walters was appointed twice, at either end of the 1980s, with his first appointment incurring the displeasure of the Conservative backbencher William van Straubenzee after Walters had publicly made disparaging comments about the "wets". Having received an admonishing letter from Straubenzee, Walters asked Thatcher's PPS, Ian Gow, what, if anything, he should say or do by way of response. Gow advised merely sending an acknowledgement via Walters' secretary, but nothing more. To assuage any injury to Walters' feelings, Gow explained that Straubenzee was "the most pompous man in the House of Commons (which is saying quite a lot) and is a leading Wet", adding that his (Gow's) wife "said to me once that she would prefer death than to be taken out to dinner by him" (TF 1981c). His second appointment in 1989, and particularly some of his comments about the government's economic policies, contributed to the resignation of chancellor Nigel Lawson, which, with hindsight, heralded the beginning of the end of Thatcher's premiership.

Each of these SPADS focused primarily on specific areas of policy, either to compensate for Thatcher's own lack of detailed understanding of specific issues (most prime ministers have insufficient time and expertise to focus on more than a couple of particular policies at any juncture) or to provide new, more radical, ideas which challenged extant departmental orthodoxies. For example, in recommending the appointment of Alan Walters as Thatcher's chief economic adviser, Alfred Sherman emphasized the need: "To cut through the miasma of unreconstructed Keynesism, intellectual evasiveness, wishful thinking and sheer muddle which pervades the Treasury and associated milieux" (TF 1980a). Walters was indeed appointed to this role, although concerns were subsequently expressed by the cabinet secretary when it was suggested that Walters should attend, and actively participate in, the meetings of the "economic" cabinet committees, given that these were normally attended only by relevant ministers and senior civil servants. This highlighted the somewhat constitutionally ambiguous nature of SPADs, in terms of the extent to which they were simply temporary civil servants or whether they were *sui generis* (NA 1982a).

Meanwhile, Ferdinand Mount was appointed as a SPAD on social policies, most notably education reform, law and order, and strengthening the traditional family. Or as Thatcher explained when outlining Mount's role to him: "Education is only part of it. What we really have to address are the values of society … to restore standards of conduct and responsibility" which were deemed to have declined since the 1960s: "Ferdy, it has to stop" (quoted in Mount 2008: 287–8). Mount himself discerned that all these policy spheres were interlinked and should thus be addressed holistically. For example, he proposed that parents should become more actively involved in schools through the expansion of directly-elected parent-governors, and schools themselves were to be exposed to more competition and diversification, while teacher training needed to be rendered more rigorous. He also suggested reform of the secondary school curriculum, to include more emphasis on the teaching of "civics", through which pupils would be inculcated with a much better understanding of the society in which they lived, and its culture, history, institutions and laws. Although he did not directly use the term, we can discern in Mount's suggestions the partial origins of what later became the National Curriculum. When he submitted these (and sundry other) suggestions to Thatcher, in a paper titled "Renewing the Values of Society", she wrote on them "I am very pleased with these ideas" (NA 1982b).

In some instances, however, the radicalism urged by a SPAD conflicted with the more cautious or pragmatic policy pursued by the relevant minister, as was evident with regard to trade union reform, a major policy on which John Hoskyns repeatedly made clear his growing impatience with James Prior's softly-softly approach (NA 1980a, 1980b, 1980c, 1980d). Hoskyns' frustration was hardly surprising, given that he and Norman Strauss had, back in May 1978, urged Thatcher to sack

Prior as shadow employment secretary, deeming him "a deadweight of obstruction – very much like the deadweight of the unions in the economy itself" (Hoskyns 2000: 67). While she shared their frustrations with Prior's ultra-cautious approach to trade union reform, Thatcher had disregarded this advice, shrewdly judging that retaining the conciliatory Prior until after the general election would assuage the anxieties of voters who might be deterred from voting Conservative due to fear that the party would embark on a radical programme of union-bashing or class warfare.

Her resolute responses to major events

During her premiership, Thatcher presided over a few major events which, if handled differently, could have grievously weakened her authority. Almost any other prime minister might have responded in a different manner, or less successfully, to such crises, and seen their reputation tarnished as a consequence. The first five years of Thatcher's premiership saw two major events which tested her mettle, namely the 1982 Falklands War, and the 1984–85 miners' strike. Either could have proved deeply damaging to Thatcher's premiership if they had been responded to with less decisiveness and determination. Consequently, her resolute stance in both instances was crucial in reinforcing her "conviction politician" persona, and in reassuring her supporters that she could be fully relied upon to defend British interests internationally and maintain the rule of law domestically.

The Falklands War

In March 1982, Argentina launched a military invasion of the Falkland Islands (or Malvinas, as they were called in Buenos Aires), which lie some 8,000 miles away from the UK in the south Atlantic, and which the South American nation had consistently claimed should be under its political jurisdiction, as they are about 950 miles off its coastline. Some senior ministers and officials in the Thatcher government had previously been sympathetic to Argentina's claims to sovereignty, and had discretely been undertaking diplomatic discussions to explore options, which included some form of shared sovereignty between Britain and Argentina or a "leaseback" scheme whereby the British government agreed "to transfer ownership of the Islands to Argentina, on the understanding that they would simultaneously grant us a lease roughly analogous to that of Hong Kong". Thatcher, however, was implacably opposed to this proposal, such that when it was submitted to her by Lord Carrington, her hand-written comments made it clear that she "could not possibly agree to the line the foreign secretary is proposing. Nor would it ever get through the HoC [House of Commons] – let alone the parliamentary [Conservative] party" (NA 1979e).

Although diplomatic talks with Argentina continued prior to 1982, the ruling-out of the leaseback or shared sovereignty options meant that they were largely inconclusive, and often focused on other issues, such as economic cooperation. This naturally put the foreign secretary in an awkward position, because with little to offer by way of substantive options, "the Argentines are showing renewed impatience for an accelerated rate of progress … deploring the hitherto slow speed of negotiations and the lack of results". Ominously, it was reported that Argentine diplomats were "making clear that, if progress is not made soon, they may have to look to other means of achieving their purpose" (TF 1981d). In this context, the Ministry of Defence undertook its own preliminary review of Britain's military options and capability in the event of any Argentine invasion of the Falklands Islands, as well as the logistical problems of defending or reclaiming territory 8,000 miles away, and which would require naval, rather than air, supremacy (TF 1981e).

However, radical political change in Argentina in December 1981 saw General Galtieri become president, and an authoritarian right-wing military junta installed, whereupon diplomatic talks with Britain over the future of the Falklands were terminated. Instead, faced with serious economic problems and concomitant discontent among the Argentine population, Galtieri resorted to the classic political tactic of embarking on an overseas military attack to divert the population's attention and anger from domestic woes, and instead manufacture patriotic fervour against a supposed external enemy: as Shakespeare's Henry IV, on his deathbed, advises his son and heir, "busy giddy minds with foreign quarrels". Thus did Argentina's military invasion of the Falklands begin on 2 April 1982, prompting Britain to despatch a naval "task force" to reclaim the Islands, which it achieved when Argentina surrendered on 14 June.

This military victory immediately transformed Thatcher's political authority; having been one of the most unpopular prime ministers of the twentieth century (according to sundry opinion polls), and subject to rumours of an imminent leadership challenge in the Conservative Party, Thatcher's popularity soared, and expectations that she would be formally challenged by one of the party's so-called grandees immediately dissipated. Whereas only 30 per cent of the British public expressed approval of Thatcher's leadership in February 1982, this figure virtually doubled (59 per cent) by June 1982 (Ipsos MORI 2013). Her status as Conservative leader now seemed assured, and her political stature was greatly strengthened. Indeed, her enormously enhanced authority and popularity, following Britain's victory in the south Atlantic, enabled Thatcher to portray herself as a latter-day female version of Winston Churchill, while also insisting that the Falklands War had signalled to the rest of the world that after decades of post-empire decline and apparent loss of national confidence, Britain was still a major actor on the world stage, and should henceforth be treated with the utmost respect in international affairs. This, in turn, reinforced her determination to adopt a tough stance against both the Soviet Union and the European Community.

Moreover, it is widely accepted that the boost to Thatcher's popularity in the wake of the Falklands victory was a major factor in securing a landslide victory in the 1983 general election, although some academics have argued that her popularity was already increasing during early 1982 due to anticipation of imminent economic recovery. In other words, her increased support coincided with, and was only slightly reinforced, rather than caused, by victory in the Falklands (Sanders *et al.* 1987).

The 1984–85 miners' strike

In the context of the impact on Thatcher's own political stature, she was absolutely determined that she would not suffer the same fate at the hands of the National Union of Mineworkers as Heath had done a decade earlier, but for Thatcher, defying the striking miners was not simply about personal pride, it was about defending Britain from what many Conservatives viewed as politically-motivated industrial militancy and left-wing insurrection. She controversially compared the conflict with the NUM to that with Argentina of two years earlier, the implication being that Arthur Scargill was a home-grown General Galtieri whose use of physical coercion and intimidation to achieve their political objectives must be defeated for the sake of democracy, liberty and the rule of law. In this context, Thatcher insisted that having defeated "the enemy without" in 1982, it was now vital to defeat "the enemy within", although it was subsequently claimed that she was referring to militants in general, rather than coal miners specifically (TF 1984b).

The claim attracted considerable criticism, but equally, it also endeared Thatcher even more closely to many Conservative MPs and supporters in the country, with one of the latter, a businessman, writing to congratulate her, and insisting that "these wretched blackmailing communists have got to be stopped once and for all" (NA 1984). Thatcher also received fulsome support and encouragement from David Hart, an enigmatic unofficial adviser to Thatcher during the miners' strike (and fund-raising organizer of activities to defeat the strike and support working miners), who insisted that "the outcome of the strike is fundamental to your political position", because "[you are] the embodiment of everything that Scargill is trying to attack. Even a minor victory for Scargill would be a major defeat for you". Conversely, Hart advised Thatcher that defeating Scargill and "his political strike ... would be the most powerful reaffirmation of your political vision", adding that: "There is an enemy within. We are at war. ... Prosecute it with the same degree of determination and control as you exercised in the Falklands" (TF 1984c).

The careful preparations undertaken since 1979, in accordance with the recommendations enshrined in the supposedly secret Ridley Report, ensured that the second (1983–87) Thatcher government was able and willing to stand firm against the NUM in 1984–85, to the extent that the strike was called-off after a year, with ministers offering absolutely no concessions to the striking miners. The Thatcher government had unwittingly been aided by the tactical errors of the NUM's leadership itself, such as embarking on the strike in spring, when the weather was beginning to turn warmer, and thus domestic coal consumption was declining. The NUM was also politically weakened by its leadership's refusal to conduct a ballot of its members to gauge support for industrial action, which was a propaganda gift for Thatcher and her ministers, because they could repeatedly insist that the strike had no democratic mandate or legitimacy, and accuse the NUM's leadership of relying on bullying and intimidation instead of the ballot-box.

This also enabled Thatcher and her ministers to challenge the degree of support the strike had among NUM members, particularly as most miners in the Nottinghamshire coalfields continued working. Furthermore, the scale of picketing at coal mines that remained operational, and the alleged intimidation of working miners, was depicted by ministers (and the Tory press) both as a law-and-order issue, and yet more evidence of the extent to which some trade unions were led by, or relied upon, left-wing bully-boys and militants; the very opposite of genuine comradeship and workers' solidarity.

The loyalty of most Conservative MPs

Norton's (1990) study also revealed that the majority (58 per cent) of Conservative MPs were neither Thatcherites nor One Nation critics, but were loyalists whose support for Thatcher was primarily due either to admiration of her strong leadership, or because such MPs were loyal to the party itself. The Thatcher loyalists were characterized by: "Attachment to the style of leadership offered by Mrs Thatcher, with no ideological commitment", and were deemed to number between 20 and 30 MPs (Norton 1990: 49). It is difficult, however, to understand how or why these MPs could strongly admire Thatcher's dominant style of leadership if they were not also committed to her ideological objectives, because in practice, Thatcher's self-proclaimed "conviction politics" encompassed her ideological stance, the concomitant policy objectives, and the style of strong leadership deemed necessary to implement these.

Perhaps more convincing is Norton's claim that the majority of Conservative MPs in the loyalist category were actually "party loyalists", whose support in the parliamentary division lobbies was primarily derived from loyalty to the institution, rather than to the individual who led it or their eponymous ideology (Norton 1990: 53–4; see also Norton 1987: 34). Their support for individual policies could be explicated in terms of these being commensurate with traditional Conservative principles and values in general, such as competition, individual liberty, private enterprise, property ownership, and the rule of law, rather than endorsing them because of Thatcher per se. To express it another way, these MPs would have practiced loyalty to any leader who was electorally successful, and thus ensured that Britain was ruled by Conservative governments.

This clearly implied that such loyalty was conditional; that it was largely dependent on the continued electoral success of whoever was Conservative leader, and that if they failed to lead the party to victory in elections, then that support was likely to be withdrawn. The leader would need to be replaced for the sake of the party's recovery and rehabilitation in lieu of the next general election. Moreover, what Thatcher's downfall in November 1990 illustrated was that for many "party loyalists", it was not simply defeat in a general election which would prompt the withdrawal of support for the incumbent party leader, but the *likelihood* of them leading the Conservatives to a defeat in the next general election. This was one of the reasons why Thatcher suffered a grievous loss of support among Conservative MPs in the autumn of 1990, in the context of contentious policy issues, concerns about her increasingly aloof or autocratic leadership style (similar criticisms had previously been levelled against Edward Heath) and reliance on non-ministerial colleagues (such as her chief press officer and SPADS), disagreements between Thatcher, her chancellor and foreign secretary over aspects of economic and European policy, and by-election defeats in previously rock-solid Conservative seats (all briefly discussed at the beginning of the next chapter).

The underestimation and ineffectiveness of her intra-party critics

When Thatcher was first elected as Conservative leader in February 1975, many of the party's MPs were incredulous, having expected a more experienced and heavyweight candidate to be victorious in the second ballot. Her time as opposition leader was thus characterized by considerable scepticism among many Conservative MPs, both over some of her policy preferences and her forceful personality, either or both of which it was feared might alienate politically moderate or centrist voters. As one eminent historian of the Conservative Party has noted, during her early leadership and premiership, Thatcher was "an object of appalled suspicion for much of the party establishment, who continued to believe that she was an accidental aberration who would not last" (Campbell 2015: 322).

This suspicion or scepticism had various sources. For some Conservative MPs, the fear was that Thatcher was politically inexperienced, having served as education secretary, but not in any of the most prestigious offices of state: Treasury, Foreign Office, Home Office. Kenneth Clarke recalls thinking that "If you'd told me this woman would become prime minister ... I'd have thought that was ridiculous", while Michael Heseltine similarly recollects that regardless of her "fine mind", he was convinced that "this was not a leader and not someone who was going to drive us to power" (BBC2 2019a).

For others, there remained apprehension that her increasingly apparent and forcefully expressed right-wing views, and self-confessed mode of conviction politics, would result in her being compared unfavourably with the calm and avuncular persona of the 1976–79 Labour prime minister, James Callaghan. Such concerns were reinforced by the criticism that Thatcher's public-speaking voice sometimes sounded shrill or strident, which she herself acknowledged could be a problem, particularly in the noisy environs of the House of Commons. As such, Thatcher recognized the need "to learn to project the voice without shrieking", and to this end, she undertook vocal coaching lessons to soften her voice and modulate her enunciation in broadcast interviews, public speeches and parliamentary debates, and thus sound less shrill or strident (Thatcher 1995: 295; see also Aitken 2013: 214; BBC2 2019a; Clarke 2016: 102–103; Millar 1993: 275; Mount 2008: 269; Sherman Papers 1977).

Even after leading the Conservatives to victory in May 1979, her intra-party critics continued to expect her to soften her stance on various policies, due to practical circumstances or events constraining her room for manoeuvre, and thereby limiting the new government's policy options; the unforeseen "events, dear boy, events" which Harold Macmillan claimed had kept him awake at night. Yet, as we have already noted, Thatcher responded to some major events and crises with shrewdness and skill, using them as opportunities to legitimize, rather than abandon, her increasingly radical agenda. Her critics in the Conservative Party also expected her to perform a U-turn similar to

Margaret Thatcher waving to the crowd outside 10 Downing Street after her election victory in May 1979 (courtesy of Tim Graham/Alamy Stock Photo)

Heath's a decade earlier, when he had abandoned the supposedly radical policies in the Conservatives' 1970 manifesto, in the context of mounting economic problems and bitter industrial conflict, and hurriedly sought a return to consensus politics instead, thereby attempting to revive the status quo ante.

The expectation that Thatcher would emulate Heath's major change of direction was fuelled by a combination of widespread bankruptcies and consequent increase in unemployment in 1980-81, Thatcher's plummeting popularity in opinion polls, and youth riots in Brixton (south London), Chapeltown (Leeds), Handsworth (Birmingham), Moss Side (Manchester) and Toxteth (Liverpool) during July 1981: if any song captured the mood of alienation, anger and despair felt by many young people in the early 1980s, it was *Ghost Town* by The Specials, which was the Number 1 "single" for three consecutive weeks in July 1981 (BBC News online 2011; Montgomery 2011). Aware that her critics in the party were expecting a major change of direction and policies in these circumstances, Thatcher mocked them at the 1980 Conservative Party conference by declaring "You turn if you want to. The lady's not for turning" (TF 1980b).

As such, the One Nation critics of Thatcher fatally (but perhaps understandably) underestimated her drive and determination, and the extent to which she was willing to persevere in the face of obstacles and opposition. As James Prior recalled: "Those of us in cabinet who were out of sympathy with Margaret's views grossly under-estimated her absolute determination ... to push through the new right-wing policies", adding that we had "assumed that quite a bit of what Margaret claimed we would do was opposition rhetoric which would be moderated by the realities of government" (Prior 1986: 118, 112).

The intellectual coherence, ideological confidence, and organizational strength which the Thatcherites exuded, was a further major reason for the ineffectiveness of the party's One Nation critics and opponents of Thatcherism. Indeed, such Conservatives had always lauded British Conservatism for being non-ideological and non-doctrinaire, deeming this to constitute one of its chief virtues, so they were ill-equipped to responding robustly to the convictions and certainties of Thatcherite colleagues. The One Nation Tories' insistence that Conservatism had always extolled such qualities as balance, caution, consent, harmony, moderation, pragmatism and scepticism "seemed limp in the face of the certainty and confidence of the Thatcherites. Moderation was not a strong rallying cry" (Riddell 1983: 45). What had once been a key source of political strength and pride among One Nation Conservatives became a serious weakness under Thatcherism (on the inexorable decline of One Nation Conservatism under Thatcher and subsequently, see Dorey & Garnett 2015).

Certainly, the One Nation Conservatives hankered after many of the policies which had characterized the postwar middle way or social democratic consensus, and so rather than abandon them altogether as Thatcherites fully intended, the wets hoped that they could be modified and ultimately salvaged. This meant that although they sometimes acknowledged the validity of *some* Thatcherite reforms, they were often motivated by different longer-term goals. For example, all Conservatives could agree on the need to reform (curb) the trade unions, but whereas the Thatcherites wanted to eviscerate the unions, to the extent that they would be permanently excluded from policy making, and thus rendered politically irrelevant, One Nation Tories envisaged that if trade union power could be tamed, thereby rendering the unions more moderate and responsible, then there could be a revival of the neo-corporatist modes of partnership symbolized by the National Economic Development Council; union reform could presage their rehabilitation (Baldry 1985; Patten 1983: 128–9; Pym 1985: 160–62, 182).

Similarly, whereas Thatcherites emphatically rejected the governmental pursuit of incomes policies as a mode of pay determination to curb inflation, One Nation Conservatives hoped that once trade unions had been reformed and were suitably chastened and contrite, there could be a return to some form of negotiated incomes policy, rather than wages being determined solely by the free market in which the strongest workers or unions secured the highest pay increases.

The One Nation Tories' criticisms of Thatcherite radicalism, and their continued belief in consensus, conciliation and compromise (reflecting their rejection of ideology), naturally attracted the contempt of Thatcher and her closest admirers and colleagues. She condemned them as "political calculators who see the task of Conservatives as one of retreating gracefully before the left's inevitable advance" (Thatcher 1993: 104), while Norman Tebbit described them as "the weaker willed, the craven-hearted, and the embittered failures amongst the Conservative Party" who "hoped she [Thatcher] would go away and let them go back to their old ways" (Tebbit 1988: 180). Nicholas Ridley was equally dismissive, claiming that Thatcher's One Nation critics "yearned for the old politics of fudge, consensus and compromise" (Ridley 1991: 175).

In the early years of Thatcher's premiership, there were occasional allegations that some of the One Nation Conservatives were collaborating to derail Thatcherite policies, reflecting their stubborn "reluctance to admit that postwar Conservative Orthodoxies can have been so hopelessly wrong". Thatcher was thus warned, in early 1980, that: "Contacts between dissenting ministers and the King Across the Water [Heath] have been increasing in frequency of late", and that there was "an organised Heathite whipping-in and press-briefing network with which Prior is associated, run by Christopher Patten – who still works closely with Gilmour – Waldegrave, Nick Scott … among others" (TF 1980c). A few weeks, later, however, Thatcher was given an update, in which it was suggested that "the main leadership and inspiration of the anti-Thatcher faction came from Prior, not from Heath", and with Chris Patten acting as "chief whip of the faction", albeit receiving "moral and political support by Prior, Mark Carlisle … Gilmour" (TF 1980d).

The weakness of the non-Conservative opposition

The weakness of the One Nation Tories inside the parliamentary Conservative Party was compounded by the ineffectiveness of the other main political parties in opposing Thatcherism, namely Labour, the Liberals, and the Social Democratic Party. This ineffectiveness derived from two sources. First, Labour's response to the post-1979 consolidation of Thatcherism was to move decisively to the left, under the influence of Tony Benn, who was idolized by many grassroots activists and younger party members as a "true" socialist. One of Benn's enthusiastic admirers was Jeremy Corbyn – first elected as a Labour MP in 1983 – who was similarly venerated by many left-wing activists and social justice campaigners as Labour Party leader from 2015 to 2019, but like Benn, alienated many mainstream and working-class Labour supporters with his radicalism and support for various controversial political campaigns and social movements. The Bennite left argued that the plethora of problems facing Britain in the late 1970s and early 1980s derived from a crisis of capitalism, and thus the ideological exhaustion of "labourism" as the party's dominant philosophy (Coates 1980: ch. 7; Miliband 1972: ch. 10). They thus insisted that the Labour Party urgently needed to adopt a much more radical and explicitly socialist programme, and in so doing, provide an ideological counterweight to the conviction politics of Thatcherism; in effect, put clear red water between the Labour Party and the Conservatives, that water having been muddied during the bipartisan policies of the pre-1979 consensus era. Yet as the 1983 general election result showed, most of the British electorate, including swathes of the working class, emphatically rejected the left-wing programme offered by Labour, convinced that the policies offered were either extreme, unaffordable or impracticable (as was also the case in 2019).

The 1983 election result saw Labour's share of the vote slump to just 27 per cent, compared to the 44 per cent achieved by the Conservatives. It should also be noted that in this election, Labour's leader, Michael Foot, compared very unfavourably to Margaret Thatcher, because not only was he deemed left-wing, he was also a prominent opponent of nuclear weapons at the height of a renewed Cold War and the perceived military threat posed by the Soviet Union. Furthermore, he was an intellectual who wrote biographies, and actually lived in Hampstead (which, for many Conservatives, ranks alongside Islington as a north London bastion of middle-class, *Guardian*-reading, left-wing intellectuals and the *bien pensant* liberal "chattering class"). He was also (again like Jeremy Corbyn, 36 years later) *not* widely viewed as prime ministerial in terms of personal style and leadership qualities, such as political decisiveness and envisaged ability to cope under pressure or in a national crisis. Needless to say, Foot compared very unfavourably with the strong and decisive leadership offered by Margaret Thatcher, especially after the Falklands War.

The second reason for the ineffectiveness of the opponents of Thatcherism beyond the Conservative Party was that it was electorally and institutionally divided between the Labour Party, the Social Democratic Party (SDP), and the Liberals. The SDP had been formed in 1981 by a group of Labour MPs and ex-ministers (joined by one Conservative MP deeply disillusioned by Thatcherism) who were strongly opposed to the move to the left after the 1979 election defeat. Still hankering after the centrist politics of the pre-1979 consensus, the SDP aimed to appeal electorally to middle-of-the-road voters who were alienated by both Bennite socialism and Thatcherite Conservatism. Initially, this strategy seemed likely to prove successful, because in December 1981, a Gallup poll indicated that the SDP and the Liberals enjoyed the support of 50.5 per cent of the British public, whereas Labour and the Conservatives each languished on 23 per cent. Yet by the 1983 general election, the SDP–Liberal Alliance – fielding just one candidate between them in each constituency, to avoid splitting their support between two candidates – polled just 25 per cent of votes cast, and whilst this was not far behind the Labour Party's poor performance, the vagaries of Britain's simple plurality of first-past-the-post electoral system meant that the Alliance only won 23 parliamentary seats, compared to Labour's 209. Moreover, although Labour and the SDP–Liberal Alliance attracted 52 per cent of all votes cast, this support was divided between the parties, whereupon the Conservative Party was elected with a 144-seat majority in the House of Commons with 44 per cent of votes cast.

This result naturally strengthened Thatcher's position and authority, and convinced her supporters that this was both a ringing endorsement of Thatcherite policies and radicalism, and that they were likely to be in government for many years to come, given the divisions and disarray among their political opponents. Consequently, the magnitude of the 1983 election victory, and the weakness of the political opposition, served to boost and entrench Thatcherism, and presaged its increased confidence (or arrogance) and radicalism: "opposition disarray enhanced Margaret Thatcher's authority, and she knew how to use it" (Biffen 2013: 421; see also Garnett & Gilmour 1996: 84).

Thatcher's authority and dominance in the Conservative Party during the 1980s was therefore a consequence of endogenous and exogenous factors, coupled with her successful response to various crises and challenges which might have undermined any other leader. Although only a minority of Conservative MPs fully shared her ideological views and objectives, the majority of them supported Thatcher due to her strong leadership and electoral success. Meanwhile, the One Nation Tories (the wets) were unable to offer a credible or convincing alternative programme, due largely to their continued hankering for many of the consensus policies of the pre-1979 era. However, these factors also contributed to Thatcher's own hubris as the 1980s progressed, as she became increasingly convinced of her own political infallibility and unassailable leadership. This attitude, and some of her associated policy decisions or public comments, actually presaged a fatal loss of support among Conservative MPs and ministers by November 1990, to the extent that she was persuaded, reluctantly, to resign.

5

The Thatcherization of the Conservative Party since 1990

As Thatcher discovered in the autumn of 1990, a hitherto dominant party leader and prime minister can suffer a catastrophic loss of support from former party loyalists due to serious policy disagreements entailing high-profile clashes with senior ministers, plummeting opinion poll ratings, by-election defeats, and/or a growing conviction among their party's MPs that the leader's glory days are well and truly behind them. Many of these scenarios can occur when a party leader and prime minister erroneously becomes convinced of their own political invincibility and immortality, and insistence that they are still revered by the people. In Thatcher's case, however, her hubris developed against a deteriorating economic situation characterized by rising inflation and higher interest rates following the 1986 "Big Bang" deregulation of financial services, her personal association with the widely reviled Community Charge or "Poll Tax", and her increasingly undiplomatic anti-European comments and speeches.

Yet expectations or hopes that Thatcher's resignation would herald a revival of One Nation Toryism were not realized. Instead, despite subsequent Conservative leaders initially advocating a more conciliatory, constructive and inclusive mode of Conservatism which embraced the social and cultural changes Britain had recently experienced, the party has become steadily more Thatcherite, not only in terms of its economic policies and priorities, but in terms of the ideological stance of an increasing number of Conservative MPs. From the early 1990s onwards, the One Nation Tories were not replenished by a new cohort, but were instead steadily replaced by economic liberals who shared the ideological commitment to the free market, and therefore a continuation, or even intensification, of privatization, public sector reform, restrictions on trade unions, tax cuts and welfare retrenchment.

When there has been an occasional departure from these policies, such as the part-privatized probation service being renationalized in May 2019, it was because the private sector companies operating it either suffered severe financial problems, or failed to provide a satisfactory level of service as stipulated in their contracts. Meanwhile, the higher government borrowing and pay subsidies (furlough schemes) implemented during the 2020–21 Covid pandemic was an ad hoc crisis-management response to an unforeseen and unprecedented scenario that threatened economic catastrophe, not a reversion back to pre-Thatcherite Conservatism. In neither instance did the more active or interventionist role of the state herald a formal abandonment of Thatcherite neoliberalism overall. Indeed, many Conservative MPs were highly critical of the *dirigiste* response to the Covid pandemic, and accused Boris Johnson's government of over-reacting.

One of the most notable aspects of the 2022 Conservative leadership to replace Johnson was the extent to which most of the contenders proclaimed their Thatcherite credentials, and pledged policies that would further entrench neoliberalism, while also promising even tougher curbs on immigration and the deportation (to Rwanda) of asylum seekers. Indeed, when the leadership contest reached its final stage, a run-off between Liz Truss and Rishi Sunak, they effectively competed to convince the party's mass membership, which casts the final vote, about which of them was the most Thatcherite.

Challenges to Thatcher's leadership

In November 1989 a so-called stalking-horse candidate – or as the then chief whip described him, "a pilot fish, which the bigger fish would watch and possibly follow" (Renton 2004: 29) – Sir Anthony Meyer, challenged Margaret Thatcher's leadership of the Conservative Party. He was a hitherto low-profile One Nation Conservative who had become increasingly concerned at Thatcher's radical policies and their ideological underpinning, but it was "her manifest distaste for everything that emanates from Europe that finally decided me to launch my challenge". However, from the outset, Meyer had "lived in the constant expectation that long before the closing day for nominations ... more redoubtable challengers would have appeared on the scene" (Meyer 1990: 162, 163).

None did so, which meant that Meyer was the only candidate standing against Thatcher in November 1989.

Thatcher attracted the support of 314 Conservative MPs, compared to Meyer's 33 votes, although 27 Conservative MPs abstained or spoilt their ballot papers. Not surprisingly, while Thatcher and her acolytes interpreted this as an emphatic endorsement of her leadership and policies, critics highlighted that a total of 60 Conservative MPs had *not* voted for her, which begged the question of how many votes might be won by a more prominent and credible leadership challenger: one of the party's "big beasts"? Her PPS, Mark Lennox-Boyd warned that about 50 of the Conservative MPs who voted for Thatcher had done so reluctantly, and that "if another 50 of your supporters become reluctant, your position becomes vulnerable" (TF 1989a).

More significant were the conclusions of a post-mortem conducted by her campaign team, which noted that despite Thatcher's emphatic victory over Meyer, reservations about her leadership were growing. Ian Gow, her former PPS and a close confidante of hers, confirmed that: "Quite a number of people voted for the prime minister with considerable reluctance ... We would be mistaken if we thought that there was enthusiasm from everybody who voted for Mrs Thatcher". He acknowledged that if the economic situation continued to deteriorate in the next year, then Conservative MPs in marginal seats might become convinced that a change of leadership was needed to prevent defeat in 1992. Apart from concerns about the general economic situation, and Thatcher's increasingly outspoken criticism of Europe, Gow cited concerns (which, he emphasized, he did not personally share) that Thatcher's leadership style was becoming too aloof or autocratic, and that as a consequence, she was "not accessible as she might be" to Conservative backbenchers.

Her lack of accessibility was also acknowledged by Lennox-Boyd, who suggested that Thatcher was perhaps too influenced by her SPAD on foreign affairs, Charles Powell, and was often overseas on diplomatic visits and attending international summits. These absences meant that she was not visible or available in the House of Commons' tea-room to talk informally with Conservative backbenchers, listen to their concerns, and perhaps assuage their anxieties: "We have got to put a stop to it" Lennox-Boyd also reported concern among Conservative backbenchers that there were "personality tensions within cabinet and that these must be resolved if confidence is to be restored. In particular,

Geoffrey Howe must be seen and treated as the PM's right-hand man". Also concerned about Powell's apparent influence on Thatcher was Tristan Garel-Jones, who had recently served as deputy chief whip: "Charles must go", adding that "Bernard [Ingham] has to go as well". Garel-Jones even suggested that: "We are talking about the beginning of the end of the Thatcher era" (TF 1989b).

Garel-Jones' words proved remarkably prescient, because a year later, in November 1990, Geoffrey Howe, having already been publicly humiliated by Margaret Thatcher when she had removed him from the Foreign Office, and half-heartedly granted him the "non-post" of deputy prime minister in July 1989 – resigned from the cabinet. The official reason was his disagreement with Thatcher's increasingly hostile stance towards Europe, and the undiplomatic language with which this was often articulated, but Howe's patience had also been exhausted by Thatcher's unconcealed contempt and cavalier attitude towards him throughout her premiership.

Thatcher characteristically sought to minimize the significance of Howe's resignation, claiming that it was ultimately a disagreement over policy style, rather than substance, but this antagonized him even more. He consequently made a devastating "resignation speech" in the House of Commons, wryly suggesting that "I must be the first minister in history who has resigned because he was in full agreement with government policy". It was the end of his speech, however, that was most significant with regard to Thatcher's leadership, because having ridiculed her attitude towards Europe – "the nightmare image sometimes conjured up … [of] … a continent that is positively teeming with ill-intentioned people scheming [against Britain]" – Howe declared that: "The time has come for others to consider their own response to the tragic conflict of loyalties with which I have myself wrestled for perhaps too long" (Hansard 1990, Vol. 180, cols 463, 465).

The following day, Michael Heseltine announced that he was challenging Thatcher for the leadership of the Conservative Party, aiming to appeal not only to pro-European Conservatives, but also the party's MPs who wanted the deeply unpopular Poll Tax replaced. The first ballot was a simple choice between Thatcher and Heseltine, as other potential candidates awaited a second ballot before declaring their own candidature. In most cases, these putative challengers were themselves cabinet ministers, and effectively obliged to declare their support for

Thatcher, while publicly denouncing the divisive and diversionary leadership contest prompted by Heseltine. Yet some of them privately envisaged, even hoped, that Heseltine would secure enough support to necessitate a second ballot, whereupon they would present themselves, particularly if Thatcher resigned at this stage. This evidently seemed to be John Major's perspective, because when a journalist asked him if he intended to stand as a leadership candidate, he replied "not against her".

Although Thatcher received the support of 204 Conservative MPs in the first ballot, compared to the 152 votes cast for Heseltine (55 per cent to 41 per cent), she was four votes short of the 15 per cent majority stipulated by the party's leadership rules, thus necessitating a second ballot (for accounts of this leadership contest, see Alderman & Carter 1991; Watkins 1991). Initially, Thatcher intended to proceed to the second ballot, but some of her erstwhile supporters believed that the best way of preventing a Heseltine victory would be for Thatcher to withdraw from the contest, thereby enabling one or two senior or popular cabinet colleagues to stand against Heseltine. Of course, they could have entered the contest anyway, but probably felt susceptible to allegations of gross disloyalty if they did so.

When Thatcher announced her withdrawal from the Conservative leadership contest on 22 November 1990, she effectively paved the way for Douglas Hurd and John Major to enter the contest and thereupon, Thatcher and her acolytes hoped, prevent a Heseltine victory. Thatcher's animosity towards Heseltine was not solely because of his pro-European stance and the bitter legacy of his (January 1986) resignation as defence secretary due to strong disagreement over the future of the Westland helicopter company, but also because she strongly disliked his unashamed support for state intervention in economic and industrial affairs: the antithesis of her neoliberalism. Indeed, she considered many of Heseltine's political views and policy stances to be redolent of the Labour Party in the 1970s and 1980s: interventionist and corporatist, and thus virtually socialist (TF 1990a, 1990b; Thatcher 1993: 841).

Thatcher made clear her support for John Major, not merely because she was determined to prevent Heseltine from succeeding her, but because she assumed that Major would continue with her economic policies, and "protect her legacy" (Slocock 2019: 320). Several years later, however, she confessed to Hurd that her support for Major had been because "he was the best of a *very* poor bunch" (Hurd 2003: 404, emphasis in original). Many of her acolytes in the cabinet similarly viewed Major as both a "stop Heseltine" and a continuity candidate, with Cecil Parkinson averring that it was "important to choose a leader who would pursue the central economic policy ... John Major was the one most likely to do so", whereas if Heseltine became leader, "we would be taking a step backwards, towards the corporatist policies of the sixties and seventies", and as such, Heseltine's economic stance was a "fundamental disqualification" (Parkinson 1992: 45, 43). Other right-wing/Thatcherite cabinet supporters of Major included Michael Howard, Peter Lilley and Norman Lamont, along with the ex-minister and former Conservative Party chairman, Norman Tebbit (Major 1999: 189; Clarke 2016: 249).

The result of this ballot, held on 27 November, was John Major 185, Michael Heseltine 131 and Douglas Hurd 56. Although John Major narrowly lacked the straightforward majority (50 per cent + 1) required in the second ballot (when the requirement of a 15 per cent margin did not apply), Heseltine and Hurd both declined to continue to a third ballot, thereby allowing Major to become leader of the Conservative Party and prime minister.

The Major premiership

In spite of the assumption among Thatcher and her allies that Major was a continuity candidate who would consolidate economic neoliberalism, others in the party hoped that Major's election to the Conservative leadership would herald a return to the One Nation mode of Conservatism of the 1950s and early 1960s, and that the radicalism of the 1980s would prove to be an aberration. The expectation of a return to a more conciliatory and consensual mode of Conservatism was encouraged by John Major's early comments upon succeeding Thatcher. For example, he declared his objective of "creating a nation at ease with itself", an aspiration that was widely interpreted as a repudiation of the instability and insecurity which 11 years of Thatcherism had produced. Major also revealed that his political idol was Iain Macleod, who had been a prominent One Nation Conservative holding various ministerial and party posts in the 1950s and early 1960s, alongside other renowned senior

Middle Way Conservatives such as Rab Butler and Harold Macmillan. A further indication that Major's premiership would herald a more constructive style of governance was his pledge to place Britain "at the heart of Europe", which was interpreted as a repudiation of the growing Euroscepticism that had been a major factor (but certainly not the only one) in Thatcher's defenestration.

Yet Major's seven-year premiership was to disappoint those Conservatives who had hoped for a return to the One Nation politics of yesteryear, because despite his warm words and initially less rebarbative rhetoric, Major mostly presided over a continuation and consolidation of the Thatcherite agenda and concomitant policies (Bale 2012: 307; Burton-Cartledge 2021: ch. 3). Just as Thatcher's apparent quoting of St Francis of Assisi's "where there is discord, may we bring harmony" was totally contradicted by her confrontational style of leadership and the divisive impact of many of her governments' subsequent policies (we say "apparent" because some theologians have claimed that St Francis himself never actually spoke these words) so was Major's allusion to a more compassionate and consensual mode of Conservatism belied by the extent to which most of his governments' economic, industrial and social policies signified an entrenchment of Thatcherism, as evinced by such policies as:

- Privatization of British Coal in 1994 and British Rail in 1996.
- The continued pursuit of free-market and supply-side economic policies.
- Further curbs on the activities of trade unions, to strengthen managerial authority and extend "labour market flexibility".
- Continued public sector reform, via more marketization, managerialism and the publication of league tables highlighting the performance of various public services and institutions, both locally and nationally. Repeated cash limits or pay freezes in the public sector, in order to curb increases in public expenditure and control inflation.
- A further tranche of coalmine closures and associated redundancies, in lieu of privatization.
- The 1993 abolition of the National Economic Development Council (NEDC), established in 1962 to promote "one nation" partnership between ministers, the TUC and employers' leaders.

- The 1993 abolition of wages councils, established in the early twentieth century to provide a minimum wage in specific jobs and industries renowned for low pay and poverty wages.
- More curbs, and stricter eligibility criteria, imposed on welfare claimants and recipients.
- The 1993 inauguration of the Child Support Agency (CSA), to secure savings in social security benefits paid to unmarried mothers.
- An intensification of the law-and-order agenda, and Major's claim that "we should understand a little less, and condemn a little more".
- A renewed moral agenda to promote marriage and traditional family values, as symbolized by Major's "back to basics" speech at the 1993 Conservative Party conference.

The other fundamental policy issue which indicated that Thatcherism had *not* been abandoned by Major's governments was the degree of Euroscepticism at all levels of the parliamentary Conservative Party, which therefore caused increasingly deep and damaging divisions in the 1992–97 Major government. Although Major's cabinet contained some prominent pro-Europeans, such as Kenneth Clarke, Michael Heseltine, Douglas Hurd, and (until losing his Bath seat in the 1992 general election) Chris Patten, it also included renowned or increasingly prominent Eurosceptics, most notably Michael Howard, Peter Lilley, Michael Portillo and John Redwood. Perhaps more important and influential, however, were the increasingly vocal and seemingly well-organized Eurosceptics on the Conservative backbenches during Major's premiership, such as Sir Richard Body, John Budgen, Bill Cash, George Gardiner, Teresa Gorman, Bernard Jenkin, Tony Marlow, Teddy Taylor, John Townend and Iain Duncan Smith.

Many of these Conservative MPs (along with several others) became known as "the Maastricht rebels", due to their vehement and active parliamentary opposition to ratification of the 1992–93 Maastricht Treaty which formally established the European Union, and whose policy objectives included plans for a single European currency by 1997 (what became the euro). Their influence over Major greatly exceeded their numerical strength, because the Conservative Party had been re-elected in 1992 with a parliamentary majority of just 21 seats, which fell further each year due to by-election defeats and the defection of some disillusioned MPs to other parties, such as Alan Howarth to New Labour and Emma Nicholson to the Liberal Democrats. This meant that in divisions (votes) in the House of Commons to ratify the Maastricht Treaty, Major's government was extremely vulnerable to defeats if/when these "rebels" either abstained, or voted against ratification. This served to embolden them, and in so doing, raised the profile of Euroscepticism in the Conservative Party.

The ideological trajectory of Conservative leaders since the Major premiership

After Major's resignation as Conservative leader following New Labour's landslide victory in the 1997 general election, a pattern became established whereby subsequent Conservative leaders initially professed their commitment to modernization and the need for the party to accept that Britain had become a more socially tolerant and culturally diverse society since the 1980s. Thus did William Hague (1997–2001), Iain Duncan Smith (2001–03) and Michael Howard (2003–05), all articulate a discourse of social inclusiveness and acceptance of diversity at the start of their respective tenures as Conservative leader, although this fell considerably short of advocating a return to One Nation Toryism. Then, when the Conservatives continued to flatline in the opinion polls, this ostensibly modernizing and progressive agenda was swiftly jettisoned, as they hastily reverted to more familiar and comforting Thatcherite tropes about further curbs on immigration, more tax cuts, a tougher stance on law and order, new crackdowns on social security fraud, and yet more denunciations of the European Union. The latter was increasingly depicted as a fledgling European superstate or nascent United States of Europe which threatened to reduce Britain to the status of a mere administrative unit or province of Brussels (for such dire warnings, see Redwood 1999: 29, 33).

This repeated reversion to Thatcherite rhetoric and advocacy of associated policies, was largely motivated by a concern to bolster the Conservatives' core vote when the purported modernization strategy failed to yield electoral dividends. The Conservative leadership feared that the party might simultaneously fail to win-back more moderate or pragmatic voters from New Labour or the increasingly popular Liberal Democrats, while losing the erstwhile support of their right-wing base, the latter likely to abstain altogether in elections – or, later, switch to UKIP.

Yet this ideological oscillation was itself frustrating for the Conservative leadership, because not only did it fail to garner much public support as evinced by disappointing election results and opinion poll ratings, at least until 2005, it caused confusion about *what* the party actually believed in, *where* it really stood ideologically, and *who* it ultimately represented. Many (potential) voters viewed the rhetorical advocacy of modernization and social inclusion as superficial and insincere, a mere tactical ruse which the Conservative leadership did not genuinely believe in, whereas the party's Thatcherites and core electoral base perceived such rhetoric as a betrayal of the Thatcher legacy; the parliamentary leadership was succumbing to political correctness, or what is now derided as "Wokeism".

Initially, it did seem as if David Cameron's leadership of the Conservative Party would genuinely herald a shift away from Thatcherism, and back towards a more constructive or conciliatory mode of Conservatism, for having become leader in December 2005, many of his early speeches were apologies for previous Thatcherite policies, such as the disdainful treatment of the public sector, and the intolerance shown towards single parents and same-sex couples. Cameron also indicated his willingness to support "green" policies in response to the growing scientific evidence of climate change and global warming. He promoted the theme of "the Big Society" as a means of mending "Broken Britain", the implication being that he wanted to see a concerted drive to tackle poverty and social exclusion (Dorey & Garnett 2012). Many commentators in the mid-2000s – including this author (Dorey 2007) – were convinced that Cameron genuinely harked back to the One Nation Conservative tradition, particularly as his family background and kinship ties, and his Eton-Oxford education, were redolent of the privileged socio-educational origins of the pre-1970s Conservative patricians and paternalists, and, in many instances, their ethos of noblesse oblige.

However, by the time that Cameron became prime minister, in May 2010 – albeit as head of a coalition government with the Liberal Democrats – he and the cabinet were committed to a stringent austerity programme to reduce the fiscal deficit accruing from the 2008 global financial crash. His apparent commitment, in opposition, to reviving One Nation Toryism was quickly abandoned, implying that it had been rhetorical, rather than real. Instead, the Cameron premiership was therefore characterized by a strengthening of neoliberalism, entailing a further tranche of tax cuts for big business and the better-off (ostensibly to kick-start the economy and restore economic growth), more privatizations and contracting-out of public services to the private sector, significant cuts in public expenditure, additional curbs on trade unions and workers' rights, and yet more attacks on the residual welfare state to render it even leaner and meaner (Dorey 2016c; Dorey & Garnett 2016; see also Burton-Cartledge 2021: ch. 6).

The 2010–15 Cameron government's austerity programme entailed proposed cuts in government spending totalling about £80 billion, with the public sector and welfare state viewed as the obvious and irresistible low-hanging fruit. Cameron and his ministerial colleagues insisted that the austerity policies were essential, due to the urgent need to cut government borrowing and reduce the deepening deficit, yet they still managed to fund income tax cuts for the better-off by reducing the highest rate from 50 per cent to 45 per cent. In effect, welfare claimants and public sector workers (and some workers in the private sector also) endured frozen or reduced incomes as the price of keeping their jobs, whereas high-earners and millionaires enjoyed tax cuts.

Furthermore, in stark contrast to Cameron's earlier emollient rhetoric in the early years of his Conservative leadership, the tone and content of ministerial oratory during his premiership was often deeply derogatory or divisive, with welfare cuts accompanied by a "shirkers versus workers, skivers versus strivers" narrative which was clearly intended to promote divide-and-rule by encouraging hostility and resentment (the politics of envy!) among low-paid workers especially, towards the unemployed. Of course, the deployment of such dehumanizing language to denigrate welfare recipients ignored – or was ignorant of – the fact that many recipients of Universal Credit are themselves in-work, but reliant on top-up social security benefits because their wages are too low to cover their basic living costs. In effect, much of the welfare state is now effectively subsidizing employers who pay poverty wages – and also, via Housing Benefit, enriching landlords charging high rents.

The Cameron government also reinforced the Conservatives' divide-and-rule strategy by reiterating the right's trope that public sector workers had comfortable jobs-for-life, and retired early, whereupon they received gold-plated pensions, in stark contrast to the hard work, limited perks, parsimonious pensions and job insecurity endemic in the wealth-creating private sector. This narrative was clearly intended to endear the Conservatives to those who worked in the private sector, and thus legitimize the renewed cuts imposed on the public sector and the harder work demanded of those employed within it.

The energy and enthusiasm with which Cameron's government pursued its austerity programme, with the poor and the public sector bearing the brunt of the cuts and ensuing financial hardship, and further savings gleaned from more privatizations and contracting-out of public services, clearly constituted a consolidation of Thatcherism (Dorey 2016c; Dorey & Garnett 2016). Cameron's support for same-sex marriage did signify his social liberalism on this particular issue, but on many others, his commitment to economic neoliberalism was evident: "Cameron accepted the Thatcherite legacy in the economic and European spheres, and is legitimately labelled as dry and Eurosceptic. His deviation from, and transcending of, Thatcherism was in the social sphere" (Heppell 2014: 178).

Theresa May's premiership

Cameron's successor, Theresa May did seem to be a more genuine One Nation Conservative, having previously warned delegates at the 2002 Conservative Party conference that they were acquiring a reputation as "the nasty party" – although many Thatcherites would doubtless take this as a compliment. Upon becoming Conservative leader in July 2016, May strongly condemned excessive boardroom salaries and bonuses in the context of recent austerity for much of the population and ever-widening inequality, and claimed that her political priority was to support those who were financially "just about managing" (soon referred to colloquially as "the jams"). She acknowledged "the divisions that we see around us, between a more prosperous older generation and a struggling younger generation; between the wealth of London and the rest of the country; between the rich, the successful and the powerful, and their fellow citizens", and thus decreed that "the central challenge of our times is to overcome division and bring our country together, by ensuring everyone has the chance to share in the wealth and opportunity on offer in Britain today" (May 2017).

This was to be achieved partly through the "shared society", whereby individual rights and freedoms would co-exist with "the bonds of family, community, citizenship and strong institutions", entailing a stronger emphasis "on the responsibilities we have to one another". This was a clear repudiation of Thatcher's "no such thing as society" claim, for it posited instead the vision of citizens who had mutual and reciprocal rights and responsibilities, redolent of earlier Conservative notions of an organic society. Indeed, May complained that "responsibilities to the people around us … have been forgotten as the cult of individualism has taken hold", because an "individualistic world can sometimes loosen the ties that bind our society together". May therefore insisted that "the central tenet of my belief – the thing that shapes my approach – is that there is more to life than individualism and self-interest" (May 2017). The rhetorical rejection of Thatcherism and three decades of neoliberal nihilism could not have been starker or more striking.

However, the relatively short duration of May's premiership, and its debilitating domination by Brexit and associated attempts at managing intra-party divisions over the details of Britain's departure from the EU, meant that her professed commitment to a One Nation policy programme yielded few, if any, discernible achievements (Dorey 2023). Even when the party's 2017 manifesto did pledge concrete One Nation policies, such as workers on the boards of companies, they were subsequently diluted or abandoned, due to lack of support among the Conservative Party's numerically dominant (economic) neoliberals and free-market fundamentalists, and also antipathy from many companies themselves, who viewed even a couple of token worker-directors as a potential threat to "management's right to manage". After all, they might start demanding a voice, vote or veto in determining executive pay.

Boris Johnson's premiership

May's successor, Boris Johnson, was ideologically opaque, perhaps deliberately so to maximize his electoral appeal. Certainly, his political views seemed to depend upon the context in which he was speaking, and who his audience was. He variously extolled the alleged virtues of free-market capitalism, eulogized Margaret Thatcher, and had previously proclaimed that "greed is good" (quoted in *The Guardian* 2013). During the 2020–21 Covid pandemic, he claimed that "the reason we have the vaccine success is because of capitalism, because of greed" (BBC News online 2021). Yet he also alluded to One Nation Conservatism, particularly during the 2019 election campaign and in his speeches immediately following his victory in that election, when Johnson spoke of his commitment to "levelling-up" the so-called (northern England) "Red Wall" towns and communities which had been "left-behind" during the previous decade or more, due to deindustrialization, globalization and the impact of austerity.

However, Johnson's professed levelling-up agenda, which was also supposed to provide a "Brexit dividend", certainly did not imply any reversion to direct wealth redistribution, enhanced workers' rights, a reversal of privatization, or any strengthening of the public sector. Instead, it was to be pursued primarily through promoting greater investment and infrastructure projects in parts of northern England and the Midlands, in order to foster economic growth and new employment opportunities, but beyond the proposed "stage two" Birmingham to Leeds/Manchester HS2 rail link – the planned Birmingham–Leeds line was subsequently abandoned for economic reasons – the professed levelling-up agenda was always short on details and specificity; it increasingly appeared rhetorical rather than real.

What compounded the difficulty of defining Boris Johnson's ideological stance was that soon after his emphatic victory in the December 2019 election, the economic consequences of the 2020–21 Covid pandemic effectively compelled the Treasury, via the chancellor Rishi Sunak, to embark on a programme of fiscal borrowing and subsidies to companies, via "furlough" schemes, in order to prevent widespread and catastrophic corporate bankruptcies, and the potential loss of millions of jobs, which would, in turn, plunge the British economy into one of the deepest recessions ever. However, this recourse to massive borrowing and spending certainly did not herald the intellectual abandonment of economic neoliberalism in the Conservative Party. It was widely viewed by many, if not most, of the party's MPs as a temporary, pragmatic, crisis-driven, and thus tactical, departure from neoliberal orthodoxy pending the "defeat" of the Covid pandemic, after which, there would be a return to neoliberalism, with the Treasury's 2020–21 financial borrowing repaid by another tranche of austerity measures involving yet more cuts in social provision and public services. This, of course, posed major problems for Johnson's professed levelling-up agenda. Furthermore, his chancellor, Rishi Sunak, subsequently confessed that he had transferred funds ostensibly designated for socio-economically deprived "left behind" northern communities to more prosperous Conservative-voting towns in southern England (Syal 2022).

The election of Liz Truss as Conservative leader

When Boris Johnson resigned as Conservative leader in July 2022, mired in controversy and scandals, and having seen over 50 ministers, parliamentary private secretaries and party officials resign between 5 and 7 July, he was replaced by Liz Truss, even though she had initially only attracted the support of 50 Conservative MPs in the first ballot of the party's leadership contest. Her support increased in each subsequent ballot, however, as other candidates were eliminated, until she and Rishi Sunak were presented to the Conservatives' mass membership to make the final choice: Truss won by 57.4 per cent to 42.6 per cent.

Apart from the blue-on-blue acrimony between the candidates that the summer 2022 leadership contest revealed, the most notable aspect was that it further highlighted the extent to which the Conservative Party had been well and truly "Thatcherized", as most of the candidates pledged tax cuts (or a raising of the threshold at which people began paying income tax), reinforcing Brexit, higher defence spending, and tougher curbs on immigration and deporting asylum seekers to Rwanda, with some also expressing doubts about extant environmental policy and plans to shift towards a green economy (in the midst of a summer when the temperature in London reached 40°C for the first time ever). The least Thatcherite candidate, Jeremy Hunt, was eliminated in the first ballot.

When Truss and Sunak had reached the final stage of the leadership contest, they sought to woo the Conservative Party's 160,000 members by proudly proclaiming their Thatcherite credentials, the main policy difference between them being over the timing of income tax cuts; Truss promising immediate reductions, whereas Sunak pledged lower taxes once government borrowing (caused by Covid) and inflation had been reduced. Truss was the clearly preferred choice of the Conservatives' mass-membership.

It was not only her policy pledges in the 2022 Conservative leadership that marked Truss as a Thatcherite, but also her co-authorship, a decade earlier, of *Britannia Unchained*, a 2012 "manifesto" advocating a further tranche of neoliberal policies and reforms, more deregulation, and a renewal of entrepreneurialism and business innovation to fuel economic growth and generate wealth. Giving the impression that the previous 30 years of globalization, labour market flexibility, managerial empowerment, privatization, relentless attacks on welfare provision, and (direct) tax cuts had never happened, the co-authors of *Britannia Unchained* – alongside Truss were Kwasi Kwarteng, Priti Patel, Dominic Raab and Chris Skidmore – bemoaned the parlous state of the British economy, particularly when compared to the apparently dynamic economies and entrepreneurship exemplified by Brazil, Canada, China, Israel, Silicon Valley (California) and Singapore. However, what attracted most attention was the claim that: "Once they enter the workplace, the British are among the worst idlers in the world. We work among the lowest hours, we retire early, and our productivity is poor. Whereas Indian children aspire to be doctors or businessmen, the British are more interested in football and pop music" (Truss *et al.* 2012: 61). Although Truss claimed, during the 2022 leadership contest, that she had not personally written these words, she did subsequently claim that many British workers needed to practice "more graft" and application to their work, and that there needed to be a change in Britain's "working culture". Her comments were fully endorsed by her business secretary Jacob Rees-Mogg (*Mail on Sunday* 2022; *Daily Mail* 2022).

Upon becoming leader and prime minister, Truss appointed Kwarteng as chancellor of the exchequer, whereupon he announced a mini-Budget which pledged that the top rate of income tax (45 per cent) would be abolished, while the basic rate would be reduced to 19 per cent. The erstwhile cap on bankers' bonuses was also to be removed. Kwarteng also announced that trade unions would face further statutory restrictions on their ability to pursue strikes; a pledge clearly intended to have a populist appeal following a summer and early autumn which had seen a wide range of workers – but especially train drivers – pursuing industrial action, as inflation greatly exceeded pay offers and eroded living standards.

Yet Kwarteng's mini-budget attracted widespread criticism, not least from institutions *not* known for harbouring left-wing views, with the International Monetary Fund (IMF) among those condemning it. What particularly alarmed such critics and other financial commentators, was that the new Truss government was intending to fund these tax cuts by borrowing up to £70 billion (although some of the money was also intended to provide financial support for people struggling with escalating fuel bills), and imposing a new period of austerity, with one cabinet minister, Simon Clarke, criticizing "the very large welfare state" (*Sunday Times* 2022).

Moreover, there was widespread concern that the tax-cuts – which Kwarteng and Truss insisted would spur economic growth, rejuvenate the British economy post-Covid and post-Brexit, and, they implied, produce a trickle-down of wealth to ordinary people – would exacerbate inflation due to the resultant increase in consumer spending, whereupon the Bank of England would feel obliged to impose further increases in interest rates. This, in turn, could have disastrous consequences for the housing market, and prove financially ruinous for home buyers who had relatively recently purchased their property when interest rates had been at their lowest for decades; some homeowners might see their mortgage payments increasing considerably at a time when food and domestic fuel prices were also rising, but pay increases were not keeping pace with these higher living costs. There was considerable anxiety that higher interest rates were likely to push Britain into a full-scale recession.

The ensuing economic panic in the City, alarm among many Conservative MPs, and opinion polls suddenly suggesting a 30-point lead for Keir Starmer's Labour Party, placed Kwarteng and Truss under intolerable political pressure, to the extent that both resigned; Truss had been prime minister for only 44 days. She was replaced as Conservative leader and prime minister by Rishi Sunak.

Thatcherization and the changing demographics of the Conservative Party

Although Norton's 1990 study of the ideological stance of Conservative MPs and ministers revealed that the 19 per cent of Thatcherites only very slightly exceeded the number (18 per cent) of One Nation critics of Thatcher(ism) – even after prominent One Nation Tories like Ian Gilmour, James Prior and Francis Pym had departed the House of Commons – the parliamentary party steadily became more Thatcherite after Thatcher's resignation; the widely anticipated post-Thatcher revival of One Nation Conservatism never materialized. On the contrary, the most notable feature of successive cohorts of Conservative MPs was their Thatcherite outlook on economic issues. For an increasing number of them, neoliberalism was the default stance, and their yearning for more cuts in direct taxation, more marketization of public services, more privatization and deregulation, more trade union reform, and yet more curbs on welfare entitlement and provision, was insatiable (on the hegemony of neoliberalism in Britain since the 1980s, see Dorey 2022).

The prolific research on Conservative MPs conducted by Tim Heppell has confirmed the increasing preponderance of Thatcherite – or economically dry (as opposed to wet) – MPs since the 1990s, particularly regarding their economic views and values. He notes that whereas the balance between Thatcherites and One Nation Tories among Conservative MPs in 1997 was 56.8 per cent and 24.5 per cent respectively (the remainder being "agnostic" or ideologically ambiguous), by 2010, the corresponding figures were 81 per cent to 13.5 per cent (Heppell 2013, 2020; Heppell & Hill 2009). Put starkly, four out of every five Conservative MPs elected in 2010 were, on economic issues at least, Thatcherites/neoliberals. As such, the main attitudinal or ideological divisions in the parliamentary Conservative Party during David Cameron's 2010–15 premiership were over Britain's membership of the European Union, and social or moral issues, most notably same-sex marriage (Heppell 2013).

It was noted in Chapter 1 how Thatcher's election as Conservative leader reflected, and then reinforced, the rise – and revolt – of the petite bourgeoisie and provincial middle class, sections of British society which had become especially aggrieved at the levels of inflation and taxation in Britain in the 1970s, the apparent power of the trade unions and working class, and the perceived moral decay and social breakdown (see Hutber 1977; King & Nugent 1979; Thompson 1980: 39–48). This, in turn, has reinforced the ideological shift away from One Nation paternalism and its pursuit of consensus and social harmony, and instead towards economic neoliberalism, conviction politics and acquisitive or competitive individualism, often suffused with a strong strand of social (and populist) authoritarianism.

For example, in terms of educational backgrounds, a declining number of Conservative MPs have been educated at Eton; whereas 75 (out of 343) of the party's 1955 intake of MPs had been educated at Eton, this number has steadily declined, falling to 47 (out of 277 Conservative MPs) in October 1974, and thence to just 19 in 2010 (out of 306) (on this decline of Old Etonians, see Wigmore 2014). There has also been a more general decline in the number of Conservative MPs previously educated at a private (fee-paying) school, from 73 per cent in 1979 to 44 per cent in 2019. During the same period, the number of Conservative MPs educated at Oxford or Cambridge University (Oxbridge) also declined, from 49 per cent to 29 per cent. As the number of Conservative MPs educated at Eton and other fee-paying schools has steadily diminished, so the number attending either a grammar or a comprehensive school has correspondingly increased: 16 per cent and 37 per cent respectively in 2017.

In the 2022 Conservative leadership contest, Liz Truss emphasized her upbringing in Leeds, and the comprehensive school education she received there, clearly trying to differentiate herself from the very much more privileged socio-educational background of her rival Rishi Sunak. On the other hand, she criticized her old school by alleging that it had not done enough to encourage poorer students to succeed academically, and as such, effectively berated her former teachers for not doing enough to promote opportunities and raise expectations. Indeed, two years earlier – with a clear nod to Thatcher's condemnation of "political correctness" in the classroom – Truss had claimed that: "While we were taught about racism and sexism, there was too little time spent making sure everyone could read and write" (*Yorkshire Evening Post* 2020). Yet Truss attended secondary school during the Thatcher–Major premierships, so the implication that she was subject to left-wing or politically-correct propaganda is unconvincing, as the National Curriculum was a Conservative initiative.

These changes in the educational backgrounds of many Conservative MPs have underpinned attitudinal and ideological changes, because the former One Nation ethos of noblesse oblige or duty of care towards the less well-off, was most prevalent among more aristocratic Conservatives and/or those who married into wealthy families. These were often the

Conservatives who were most likely to have attended Eton, not least because their parents could afford the annual fees, which in 2022–23 were £46,296. Through the ethos of noblesse oblige, many of those emanating from elite socio-economic and educational backgrounds were inculcated with a strong sense of civic duty and public service, and taught, via their parents and/or their education, that their privileges entailed corresponding responsibilities.

Clearly, not *every* Conservative who attended Eton was/is a One Nation Tory (as noted above, we would not classify David Cameron as such, nor Boris Johnson), and not *every* grammar school-educated Conservative is an individualistic and neoliberal Thatcherite (Theresa May being a good, but rare, example of a grammar school-educated One Nation Tory), but in general, there has been a strong correlation between an aristocratic or otherwise elite background, a prestigious public school education and a One Nation stance, and equally, a preponderance of neoliberals and/or Thatcherites among those Conservatives who have emanated from more modest, middle-class backgrounds, and attendance at a grammar or comprehensive school. The latter category have generally viewed themselves as evidence of the success that can be achieved by individual effort and personal ambition, and as a consequence, their attitude is often: "We made it, so almost anyone can make it if they really want to and try hard enough. If they fail to do so, it is probably their own fault, not society's".

Broadly speaking, the two variants have symbolized the contrast between, on the one hand, the ethos of noblesse oblige and society viewed as an organic entity which enshrines reciprocal duties and responsibilities between its constituent classes and civic institutions, and on the other, a meritocratic society (if a collective entity such as "society" is even acknowledged) based on acquisitive individualism, the pursuit of rational self-interest under the rule of law, and equality of opportunity whereby almost anyone can enjoy material success and social mobility if they work hard enough, and make the correct economic decisions and/or lifestyle choices. Needless to say, this perspective is much less sympathetic or tolerant towards the poor than the One Nation Tories, because the latter generally acknowledge their privileges and good fortune in being born into (or inheriting) wealth or having the "right sort" of family ties, expensive and elite education, and social connections.

The One Nation Conservatives – personified in the 1950s and 1960s by Harold Macmillan – constantly feared that the return of high unemployment, or the growth of excessive (albeit never defined) inequality, would weaken working-class support for capitalism and parliamentary democracy, and might ultimately result in support for radical reform or revolution. The One Nation Conservative ethos reflected Benjamin Disraeli's warning that: "The castle cannot rest if the cottage is not happy" (quoted in Monypenny & Buckle 1929: 709). Or as Ian Gilmour advised more than a century later, during the first Thatcher government, "we should be wise to remember [Edmund] Burke's remark about there coming a time when men would not suffer bad things merely because their ancestors had suffered worse" (Gilmour 1983: 7). Gilmour subsequently warned that:

> Those who are effectively excluded from the benefits of society cannot be expected to remain passive indefinitely … those who wish to 'conserve' the fabric of society and avoid the shocks of violent upheavals must look to the contentment of all our fellow countrymen. The key to the survival of any social order is its ability to satisfy the aspirations of people in all walks or layers of life … a nation can be at ease with itself only when all its citizens feel that their government takes an interest in them, and is sympathetic to their concerns. The true purpose of Conservatism is to work for harmony. (Gilmour 1992: 276, 278–9; see also Pym 1985: 143)

The diminution of the One Nation Conservatives from the 1980s onwards was the consequence of several factors: the decline of the English aristocracy or its increasing reluctance to pursue a political career, particularly in an era of declining deference; the expansion of the middle class(es) due to economic restructuring and the increase in white-collar jobs and small businesses; the growing assertiveness among sections of this middle class, coupled with a sense of grievance that their interests had been neglected, or even sneered at, by successive postwar governments and so-called *bien pensant* liberals and intellectuals; the increasing preference of Conservative constituency parties and grassroots activists to select parliamentary candidates in their own image, or who could be relied upon to sustain Thatcherite policies; the dismissal or resignation, from frontline politics, of some senior One Nation Conservatives during the 1980s (Lord Carrington, Ian Gilmour, James Prior, Francis Pym, Norman St John Stevas) and their subsequent deaths; the defection of some One Nation MPs to New Labour or the Liberal Democrats from the 1990s onwards; the creation of a short-lived centrist party by some One Nation/pro-European Conservatives during Boris Johnson's premiership (Heidi Allen, Anna Soubry and Sarah Wollaston).

As the socio-educational background of Conservative MPs has become less aristocratic and privileged, and correspondingly more middle class and seemingly meritocratic, so too have noblesse oblige and paternalism declined to the point of virtual disappearance. Very few Conservative MPs in the twenty-first century believe that their social backgrounds have imbued them with privileges that entail a corresponding moral obligation to accept a duty of care towards the less well-off. They are thus overwhelmingly hostile towards state intervention if it is intended directly to tackle poverty, promote greater equality (unless it is equality of opportunities), and pursue wealth redistribution via higher taxes or more generous welfare payments. Instead, the entrenchment of Thatcherite free-market economics and neoliberalism among the vast majority of modern Conservative MPs means that the basis or source of material success, both individually and nationally, is deemed to be hard(er) work, individual effort, labour market flexibility, lower taxes, more competition, private enterprise, the pursuit of social mobility, self-reliance, supply-side economics and weak trade unions.

6

The contradictions and consequences of Thatcherism

One of the most interesting aspects of Thatcherism is its contradictory character, and the ways in which it yielded consequences that were incompatible with much of Conservatism more generally. Certainly, many of the socio-economic problems that have increasingly afflicted Britain since the 1990s can, in large part, be attributed to the cumulative or slow-burn consequences of Thatcherite policies, which were then consolidated by John Major's (1990–97) and subsequent (post-2010) Conservative-led governments. As we noted in the previous chapter, the pursuit of economic neoliberalism and the fetishization of "the market" has continued apace long after the end of Thatcher's premiership, entrenching a British society in which individualism superseded collectivism, people were recast as consumers rather than citizens, and activities were judged primarily in terms of how profitable they were, how far the maximized shareholder values, or, most notably in the public sector, how much (economic) value they added (Dorey 2022).

Of course, the Conservatives were in opposition from 1997 to 2010, but the New Labour governments led by Tony Blair and Gordon Brown only marginally tempered some of the Thatcher–Major governments' policies, but made no significant or sustained attempt at reversing them, nor did they evince any desire to do so. With the notable exception of the statutory minimum wage, which was introduced at the rate of £3.60 per hour, only 10 pence more than the CBI had proposed, but 90 pence less than the £4.50 proposed by the TUC, the Blair governments perpetuated, and thus further entrenched, neoliberalism by continuing with the rejection of nationalization and public ownership, pursuit of supply-side economics, marketization, consumerism and hyper-managerialism in education and the NHS, retention of legislative limits on trade union activity and veneration of labour market flexibility, the transformation

Prime Minister Tony Blair shakes hands with Baroness Margaret Thatcher during a Falklands War commemoration in London, 17 June 2007 (courtesy of Anwar Hussein/ Alamy Stock Photo)

of erstwhile citizens into customers and consumers, and the *a priori* premise that the interests of big business were synonymous with the interests of civil society; market mania *maximus*.

Even the 2008 global financial crisis failed to undermine the hegemony of neoliberalism, although some on the left hoped, and some on the right feared, that it might. On the contrary, the Conservative right immediately recast the 2008 crash as a crisis of social democracy occasioned by New Labour's allegedly excessive public spending. The Conservatives' response to the 2008 financial crash constituted a clear example of "disaster capitalism", whereby the right actually welcomes an economic crisis as another opportunity to eviscerate any remaining vestiges of social democracy by legitimizing further privatizations, more contracting-out of public services, lower taxes for the better-off and large companies, another series of cuts in supposedly unaffordable social protection and support, and a renewed assault on what remains of employment protection and workers' rights (Klein 2007; Krugman 2012; Loewenstein 2015; Mirowski 2014). In effect, the response of neo-liberal Conservatives to the 2008 financial crash was to intensify the implementation of Thatcherite economic neoliberalism, anti-welfarism and demonization of the poor, and denigration of the public sector and its employees, albeit evincing a greater degree of social liberalism on issues such as same-sex marriage (although many Conservatives were bitterly opposed to this policy). However, the pursuit of Thatcherism 2.0 since 2010 has meant that its contradictions and deleterious consequences have become even starker, and negatively affected many more people, not least sections of the middle class who have previously supported, and indeed usually benefitted most from, Conservatism.

In terms of the contradictions and negative consequences of Thatcherism and its legacy of neoliberalism, four specific aspects will be explored in this final chapter: (1) the ideological character of Thatcherism in a supposedly non-ideological Conservative Party; (2) the Thatcherite attack on hitherto venerated civic institutions; (3) the contradictory consequences of specific Thatcherite policies in practice; and (4) the generally destabilizing and destructive impact of Thatcherism on individual security, settled communities, society as an organic entity, and social stability in general.

Thatcherism as an ideology in an avowedly non-ideological Conservative Party

Some critics (even within the Conservative Party, like Ian Gilmour and Chris Patten) argued that Thatcherism was incompatible with Conservatism precisely because the former was ideological, whereas Conservatism had always prided itself on its rejection of theories and abstract ideas, preferring instead to govern on the basis of empiricism, pragmatism and the experience or accumulated wisdom embodied in established institutions. This Burkean and Oakeshottian perspective rejected radical change, based on theoretical concepts or intellectual blueprints, in favour of gradualism and incrementalism. It also rejected the teleological premise of most "isms", most notably liberalism and Marxism, whereby society was assumed to be progressing ineluctably towards some emancipatory end goal, as optimistically envisaged by the philosophers of eighteenth-century Enlightenment, and sundry economists, political theorists and sociologists subsequently. According to Oakeshott (1967: 127): "In political activity, then, men sail a boundless and bottomless sea; there is neither harbour for shelter nor floor for anchorage, neither starting-place nor appointed destination. The enterprise is to keep afloat on an even keel; the sea is both friend and enemy; and the seamanship consists in using the resources of a traditional manner of behaviour in order to make a friend of every hostile occasion".

Traditional (i.e., non-Thatcherite) Conservatives also eschewed ideology because of their insistence on the imperfectability of human nature, and the extent to which people behaved according to emotions and passions, rather than pure reason. Furthermore, the traditional Conservative belief in the unequal distribution of human attributes, such as intelligence, had profound implications for the notion of a more equal or rational society. According to (arguably) the founding father of modern Conservatism, Edmund Burke (2004: 183): "We are afraid to put men to live and trade each on his private stock of reason, because we suspect that the stock in each man is small, and that individuals would do better to avail themselves of the general bank and capital of nations and ages".

Now, although Thatcherism also fully accepted that equality was neither attainable nor desirable, its intrinsic economic liberalism and veneration of consumer sovereignty did assume *a priori* that individuals were, or could be moulded (socially engineered?) into, rational economic actors or agents, who operated in the market by making decisions on a cost-benefit basis. Here, Thatcherite economics jarred with traditional Conservative philosophy and the latter's pessimistic (or realistic) premise about human rationality and cognitive limitations. If different individuals had differing degrees of intelligence, and human conduct in general was driven more by emotions and passions than by reason, then the goal of establishing a society comprised of rational consumers all making logical and well-informed economic decisions was itself utopian, and thus unattainable.

More generally, Gilmour argued that Thatcher "identified herself so closely with her beliefs that her statecraft, her instinct and her desire for hegemony cannot be separated from the ideological fervour which inspired them". He added that Thatcher was "unique among British prime ministers in ... having an 'ism', because none of her predecessors were so wedded to a set of abstract ideas". He was therefore convinced that "the nature of Mrs Thatcher's beliefs and the depth of her attachment to them still mark her down as an ideologue" (Gilmour 1992: 269, 270–71). After all, as noted in Chapter 2, Thatcher openly acknowledged the extent to which she had been influenced by the ideas and theories of figures such as Milton Friedman, Friedrich Hayek and Adam Smith, and variously cited them in sundry speeches.

Denigrating established institutions

A core feature of traditional Conservatism has been the defence of established cultural, political and social institutions, a stance adopted for three main reasons. First, they are deemed to enshrine the accumulated experience and wisdom of the past, which is then transmitted to subsequent generations, thereby contributing to overall social stability and continuity. In this regard, Conservatives consider long-standing civic institutions to represent a vital link and connecting thread between the past, the present and the future, thereby ensuring that important values, practices and traditions endure generationally. Until Thatcherism, British Conservatives had lauded the importance of institutions such as the BBC, Church of England, civil service, local government, judiciary, the monarchy, parliament and universities.

The second reason why pre-Thatcherite Conservatives revered established civic institutions is the concomitant notion of society as a complex organic entity, in which the component parts are interlinked and mutually dependent. Furthermore, the various institutions, such as the family and education system, are also crucial sources of socialization, inculcating young people, and thus the next generation, with their society's dominant values and codes of behaviour. Again, these institutions are deemed vital to the transmission of societal values to the next generation, thus ensuring overall continuity and stability.

Third, these organizations also constitute "intermediate institutions" – or what Edmund Burke (2004: 135) termed "little platoons" – which provide a buffer between the individual and the state, and also a source of identity or allegiance in addition to the nation-state. In so doing, these bodies serve to diffuse power which would become dangerous if it was concentrated in the hands of either the people en masse (the tyranny of the majority), or one major institution. Instead, Conservatives have traditionally decreed that a pluralistic plethora of cultural, legal, political and social institutions, which were partly autonomous but also partly interdependent or reciprocal in their relationships, would ensure that power was dispersed and shared more widely, and thus minimize the likelihood of tyranny accruing from the concentration of power in too few hands. According to Ian Gilmour: "It is these buffers between the individual and the state which preserve liberty by preventing a direct confrontation between them. When they are swept away, tyranny or anarchy follows. Conservative writers from Burke ... to Oakeshott have stressed the vital importance of barriers between state and citizens ... when a government endangers the freedom of the individual, such collective groupings provide an essential first line of resistance" (Gilmour 1992: 199; see also Gilmour 1978: 64; Waldergrave 2022).

For all of these reasons, non-Thatcherite Conservatives have usually insisted on the need to defend and maintain established institutions. This did not mean obstinately resisting all change, but instead insisting that any changes should be evolutionary, incremental and piecemeal, and ultimately intended to preserve or even strengthen the existing institutions; change in order to conserve. Moreover, changes should be based on practical necessity, not abstract principles or theory.

By contrast, Thatcherism increasingly proved hostile to, or impatient with, many of Britain's intermediate institutions, convinced that they were an obstacle to the radical changes that Thatcher and her acolytes were pursuing, either because they impeded the smooth operation of a free-market economy, or because they enshrined values that were incompatible with, and even hostile to, the Thatcherite veneration of commercialism, individualism, material acquisitiveness and profit-maximization. Civic institutions that Conservatives had previously deemed integral to maintaining the status quo were increasingly denigrated by Thatcherism either as "conservative" obstacles to the radical restructuring of the British economy and society, or because they had allegedly been infiltrated and colonized by Marxists who were using these institutions to disseminate left-wing values and denigrate capitalism: "Any regard for the importance of intermediary institutions in society ... was thought a denial of the government's democratic authority" (Patten 2018: 145). As such, the self-styled "Red Tory", Philip Blond, laments that: "Mrs Thatcher, by endorsing an extreme individualism, undermined and destroyed the very associative traditions that are the only protection against the state" (Blond 2010: 126).

Hence the BBC, Church of England, civil service, the "education establishment" (sometimes derided as "the blob" – a derogatory portmanteau term derived from *blo*ated *b*ureaucracy), the House of Lords, universities and Labour-run local authorities, were increasingly criticized by Thatcherites. For example, Keith Joseph lamented that "our Establishment – the church, the educational system, the universities, the civil service, the political parties" had "taught that there's something faintly discreditable about business" (quoted in Harrison 1994: 212). This, he claimed, was part of a "long-standing *trahison de clercs* in this country" (Joseph 1987: 27), whereby the "socialist ethic of institutionalised envy [was being] fostered by many politicians, communicators, and academics" (Joseph, speech to Conservative Party conference, 6 October 1976, reported in *The Times*, 7 October 1976).

The BBC, for example, was – and continues to be – denounced as Marxist, either in terms of the political views of some of its staff, or the content of sundry programmes. To Thatcherites, the BBC (the acronym sometime derided as the Bolshevik Broadcasting Corporation or the Bash Britain Campaign) has been a site of consistent, even systematic, left-wing infiltration by documentary makers, editorial staff and scriptwriters, and this alleged bias was encouraged by the fact that many of the BBC's jobs were advertised in *The Guardian*'s media supplement on Mondays, which therefore virtually ensured that staff were recruited from a narrow and very specific socio-cultural milieux – one which was invariably hostile to the Conservatives and capitalism. The appointment of such staff was then deemed to underpin a left-wing or Marxist bias both in the allegedly aggressive or hostile tone adopted by news presenters when interviewing Conservative ministers, and in the content of sundry current affairs documentaries like *Panorama*.

Similarly, the Church of England – historically characterized as "the Conservative Party at prayer" – was increasingly criticized by Thatcherites due to concerns expressed by some senior clergy over various policies or their consequences, in terms of their impact on the poorest or most vulnerable sections and communities of British society. For example, when in 1985 the Church of England published *Faith in the City*, a critical report into inner-city deprivation and destitution, one (un-named minister) denounced it as "Marxist" (Gilmour 1992:

114). Then, as today, the Church of England was berated for meddling in political affairs and displaying an anti-Conservative bias, whereupon it was exhorted to confine its public comments to ecclesiastical and spiritual matters; to "stay in the pulpit, and keep out of politics". As the Brazilian priest, Hélder Câmara, once remarked: "When I give food to the poor, they call me a saint. When I ask why the poor have no food, they call me a Communist".

Another once venerated institution, which attracted (and continues to attract) the hostility of Thatcherites was the civil service, which was invariably viewed or depicted as being an expensive and bloated bureaucracy (another "blob") staffed by risk-averse, jobs-for-life, functionaries who are also allegedly rewarded with gold-plated pensions when they take early retirement in their 50s. Moreover, they are strongly suspected of resisting and diluting radical reforms pursued by Conservative governments; in effect, Thatcherites – rather like many on the left – have variously condemned the civil service for its excessive conservatism, and consequent refusal to embrace change and modernization. Since 2016, the Conservative right has also accused the civil service of seeking to sabotage Brexit, due the allegedly pro-EU or Remain stance of many senior civil servants.

The hostility of Thatcherites to the senior civil service was readily matched by the disdain displayed towards many educationalists, and the routine denigration of teachers and university lecturers. This was part of a more general populist anti-intellectualism among Thatcherites (and in English culture more generally), who depicted themselves as purveyors and practitioners of common sense, even when intoxicated on the theories of Friedman, Hayek and (Adam) Smith. Thatcherites regularly blamed teachers for allegedly declining educational standards, failure to instil discipline in the classroom, and increasing illiteracy and innumeracy among school-leavers. According to Alfred Sherman, "the education establishment … had brought standards steadily down" since the 1960s, and continued to do so, in defiance of the reforms enacted by the Thatcher governments (Sherman 2005: 107).

Thatcher herself denounced the erstwhile Department of Education and Science for enshrining an in-house ideology that was "self-righteously socialist", and therefore promoting equality in schools as "a stepping-stone to achieving equality in society". She also complained that "too many teachers were less competent and more ideological than their predecessors" (Thatcher 1993: 166, 90). This derision of the so-called education establishment and teaching profession was echoed by Thatcher's successor, John Major, who condemned "the giant left-wing experiment in levelling-down" and "the failed nostrums of the 1960s and 1970s", which he attributed to "the fads and fashions that short-changed an entire generation of children … called … progressive education" (Major 1992: 9; 1993: 31; 1999: 7, 20; see also Baker 1993: 168; and John Patten 1995: 196-7).

There was (and remains) an ingrained suspicion among Thatcherite Conservatives that many school-teachers are irredeemably left-wing, and that pupils were therefore highly vulnerable to anti-Conservative propaganda in the classroom. Keith Joseph informed Thatcher of a "growing concern about the way in which politically controversial issues are handled by teachers in our schools and colleges" and suggested that guidance ought to be disseminated to local education authorities to ensure that pupils always received "education and never political indoctrination" (NA 1986e). One possible solution mooted by Joseph was to establish a body, such as a tribunal, whose role would be "to investigate parents' complaints that their children had been exposed to political views in a manner which was not responsible" (NA 1986f).

The same concern was, and still is, harboured about higher education, with Thatcherites suspecting that many, if not most, university lecturers were/are Marxists, or "Marxoid dons" as Sherman liked to refer to them (Sherman 2005: 108). These supposedly ultra-leftist academics were/are suspected of indoctrinating impressionable students with left-wing views, particularly through the proliferation of humanities and social science degrees, and modules in subjects such as critical theory, gender studies, peace studies, political science and, of course, sociology. Thus did Sherman condemn "the Marxoid domination of social studies" before asserting that political science was "an oxymoron" (Sherman 2005: 69, 81). Meanwhile, Hayek lamented "the domination of University bookshops by left-wing paper backs", to which Joseph responded by suggesting that the Centre for Policy Studies and the Institute of Economic Affairs might aim to fill this gap in publications which extolled "a free society" (TF 1975g). Meanwhile, in 1983, during Keith Joseph's tenure as education secretary, the Social Science Research Council was renamed the Economic and Social Research Council, thereby pointedly removing the word science from its nomenclature.

This jaundiced view of academics and the social sciences was reinforced by the involvement of many students and graduates in sundry social movements and protests which burgeoned in the latter half of the 1960s, most notably those campaigning against racism and sexism, and opposing the United States' anti-communist military intervention in Vietnam; Thatcher referred to such protests as "kindergarten Marxism" (Thatcher 1995: 185). Those who were inclined to accept these caricatures of ultra-left-wing academics unduly influencing or corrupting their students, might have had their fears compounded by the 1975 publication of Malcolm Bradbury's *The History Man*, a brilliant satire of academic life, depicted through the anti-authority attitudes, bohemian lifestyle, and morally dubious activities, of its leading character, Howard Kirk, a sociology lecturer (naturally) who had no qualms about sharing recreational drugs with some of his tutees when hosting parties, or sleeping with his female students.

One major consequence of Thatcherism's extension of neoliberalism to higher education is the extent to which universities are now expected to focus on the apparent needs of employers and the economy, thus rendering them a core component of supply-side economics. For Thatcherite neoliberals, universities are no longer primarily about providing an advanced education through teaching and learning per se, but about the inculcation and transmission of so-called transferable skills, and fulfilling a professed employability agenda, to equip students with the attributes and characteristics that employers and corporations require, and which will contribute to the wider market economy. Consequently, today's Thatcherites are increasingly questioning the economic worth or purpose of some university degrees, which pre-Thatcherite Conservatives would have ascribed an intrinsic intellectual and cultural value.

The crude economistic or business-model approach to higher education adopted by Thatcherism naturally appalled Ian Gilmour, who argued that "universities cannot sensibly be treated like factories or evaluated by economic output indices. Free-market ideas are even less appropriate for universities than they are for health". As such, he condemned the Thatcherite assumption that "there is no essential difference between a school or university and a supermarket", insisting that: "Education is not a simple commodity [like] the purchase of vegetables or a packet of cigarettes ... cannot be bought and sold like sausages or children's clothes" (Gilmour 1992: 163, 170). Yet in the 2020s, students are widely viewed as customers or consumers, lecturers and professors are service providers imparting employment skills, and a degree is merely a commodity or product whose value is measured in terms of its contribution to the economy, or/and the salary earned by a student after graduation.

The contradictory consequences of specific Thatcherite policies

In various policy areas, the relentless pursuit of Thatcherite policies has yielded unintended consequences that have either generated new problems, or seriously undermined some of the precepts and principles of Thatcherism itself. As such, quite apart from the allegedly contradictory nature of Thatcherism per se, according to its sundry critics (including some former senior figures in the Conservative Party itself, like Ian Gilmour), it was certainly contradictory in practice, in terms of the outcomes produced by various policies.

Preaching fiscal prudence while deregulating banks and building societies

As noted in Chapter 2, Thatcherism condemned the allegedly excessive and inflationary public spending and fiscal recklessness of post-1945 British governments, and insisted on the need to restore sound money and financial prudence. In comparing the national economy to the household budget of ordinary people, Thatcher had extolled the virtues of avoiding excessive spending and borrowing, not getting into debt, and living within one's economic means; if people wanted to buy something relatively expensive, they ought to save the money for it until they could afford to pay for the item outright, unless it was a home, of course. These homilies were a further reflection of how Thatcher's family background and upbringing shaped her formative views, which were subsequently imbued with intellectual coherence and rigour by the ideas of Friedman, Hayek, Joseph, Powell, Sherman, and (Adam) Smith, but also presented as mere common sense, or what every "housewife" knew, thereby denying their ideological character.

Yet in spite of Thatcher's provincial petit-bourgeois assumptions about domestic affairs and household finances, and the extent to which these could and should shape Britain's political economy, her premiership heralded an unprecedented expansion of personal borrowing and consumer spending, due largely to the combined impact of chancellor Nigel Lawson's "Big Bang" deregulation of financial services and banking in 1986, the proliferation of credit cards which ushered in an era of "buy now, pay later", the mass (crass) consumerism unleashed in the 1980s, and the escalation of property prices.

The Big-Bang deregulation of Britain's financial services sector was itself a key component of the Thatcher governments' neoliberalism, whereby private companies – in this instance, banks and building societies – were to be freed from most state-imposed restrictions on their commercial activities. After all, if the free market was self-regulating, and established its own equilibrium due to the benign guidance of the so-called hidden-hand, coupled with the immutable laws of supply and demand, then there could be no justification for political restrictions on the lending policies of banks and building societies; they should be free to sell their products and services in the same manner as any other high street retailer. This was also intended to foster competition between financial institutions, reflecting the Thatcherite assumption that: "The presence of a competitor always tightens up the quality of service and keeps prices under careful scrutiny". This, in turn, would greatly benefit customers and consumers, it being assumed that "people are, on the whole, pretty canny about their own money" and therefore "will not be tempted into Get-Rich-Quick Limited" (NA 1985).

Of course, the almost inevitable consequence was a sudden increase in borrowing by, and lending to, ordinary people, because financial credit and loans immediately became much more easily attainable and widely available, often on very favourable personal terms, as high street banks and building societies competed against each other for customers to lend money to, including, crucially, mortgages. For many people, borrowing money had never been easier or, initially, so cheap.

The ensuing increase in personal debt was greatly compounded by the vast expansion of credit cards, which was also a result of the intense competition between financial institutions for customers. Hitherto, credit cards had mainly been a financial tool of the rich, because payment by card obviated the personal risks associated with publicly carrying large sums of cash when purchasing a new car, Saville Row suit, or yacht on the French Riviera, although in the 1970s, merely getting out one's credit card was a means of displaying one's high financial status: a cultural signifier. By the mid-1980s, however, credit card ownership became commonplace, as banks similarly competed against each other, often by offering (potential) customers very good and attractive deals; a high cash limit, perhaps, or initially low interest rates, and sometimes no-interest charged on either the first £100 spent, or on the first three-months' purchases.

With remarkable irony, the ubiquity of credit card ownership, and the ease with which people could use them to make relatively expensive purchases (albeit depending on their credit limit), completely undermined Thatcherite homilies about fiscal prudence and financial restraint, both individually and nationally. Suddenly, millions of people routinely purchased day-to-day items with credit cards, thereby obviating the need to save-up enough money first: the "buy now, pay later" psyche was accompanied by an "enjoy it now, worry about the cost later" mindset. With no cash being handed over, and the credit card statement being issued monthly, it was easy – sometimes too easy – for people to spend relatively large amounts of money without fully realizing just how they had spent until their bill arrived 3–4 weeks later.

With the relatively easy availability of credit, and the concomitant ease with which many people could borrow money or pay for items on their credit card, the 1980s naturally witnessed the intensification of the consumer society. Of course, the development of mass consumerism had begun back in the 1950s and early 1960s, when car ownership, household appliances like fridge-freezers and televisions, and holidays in southern Europe, were acquired or enjoyed by an increasing number of British people, and also youth culture or "the teenager" were created or socially constructed via fashion (especially in clothing and hairstyles) and rock/pop music. However, it was during the 1980s that the consumer society became much more prominent and prevalent, as millions of people used the easy availability of credit (cards) and bank loans to buy new cars and furniture, and pay for home improvements.

The other consequence of financial deregulation and easier or (initially) cheaper borrowing was the expansion of homeownership. Of course, increased property-ownership was a major objective of Thatcherism – in fact, the goal of a property-owning democracy had first been mooted by Anthony Eden in 1946 – so this could be classified as a success, but the manner in which it was achieved also rather undermined Thatcher's strictures about prudence and living within one's financial means. Following the Big Bang, the intense competition among banks and building societies for customers (and inter alia new sources of profit, accrued from the interest charged on loans) resulted in a marked increase in mortgage lending as more people purchased their own homes. However, with the demand for housing often exceeding the availability or supply of available properties, the inevitable consequence was that house prices began rapidly to increase.

Initially, this made many younger people even more determined – or desperate – to clamber on to the bottom rung of the housing ladder before house prices increased completely beyond what they could just about afford, thus leaving them marooned in increasingly expensive and often insecure rental housing in perpetuity. As a result, some people financially over-extended themselves in the size of the mortgage they obtained, leaving them highly vulnerable both to the slightest deterioration in their financial circumstances and/or an increase in interest rates. The latter is exactly what occurred in the late 1980s, as the Treasury responded to the inflation fuelled by the credit explosion and surge in consumer spending based on borrowing by raising interest rates to curb the money supply and cool an overheating economy: the Bank of England's base rate rose from 9.8 per cent in May 1986 to 14.8 per cent by October 1989.

For many people who had acquired a mortgage in 1986 at the absolute upper limit of what they could then afford in terms of monthly repayments, when interest rates were just below 10 per cent, the subsequent increase in interest rates to almost 15 per cent was financially disastrous, and left some recent home-buyers unable to afford their monthly mortgage payments. Some people had their home repossessed by the bank or building society due to their mortgage arrears, thus rendering them either homeless, or consigned once again to the cost and precarity of the private rental market. The early 1990s also witnessed the phenomenon of "negative equity", whereby a recession-induced slump in property prices meant that some people found themselves living in homes whose market value was now less than the price they had paid when they bought it; they might have bought their apartment or house in 1987 for £60,000, but then found that in 1993, it was only worth

£50,000, although their mortgage costs and repayments remained the same.

The burgeoning bureaucracy in privatized industries and the public sector

We also noted in Chapter 2 how the Thatcherite critique of nationalized industries and the public sector condemned their bureaucratic character, and thus the need either to privatize them, or where that was deemed impracticable or electorally risky (as in the case of the NHS), marketize them by instilling private-sector principles and practices to improve efficiency and increase responsiveness to the preferences of their "customers". With regard to nationalized industries in particular, privatization was deemed an integral element of the Thatcherite commitment to "rolling back the state" and inter alia, the associated bureaucracy which had expanded relentlessly since 1945. Yet privatization and public sector reform have both yielded new modes of bureaucracy, such that although Thatcherites waxed lyrical about slashing red tape and "setting people free" from bureaucratic control, the decades since the 1980s have witnessed the emergence of a new "regulatory state", and in the public sector especially, the entrenchment of an intrusive, time-consuming and morale-sapping "audit culture" (Jenkins 1995; Moran 2003; Power 1997).

The Thatcherite discourse which underpinned privatization decreed that by removing major industries and public utilities from the state sector, they would be compelled to become competitive in order to attract customers, who would henceforth become their main or sole source of revenue, rather than taxpayers' subsidies. This would supposedly lead to a better service and lower prices for the public, as the privatized industries sought to maximize their customer base or market share by offering a better service or/and lower charges or fares than their rivals; standards would go up, and prices would come down. In the real world, however, privatization often proved less benign or beneficial to the public than Thatcherites anticipated, largely due to the oligopolistic character of many privatized industries and services.

Although there were ostensibly several companies in each sector, the degree of genuine customer choice and sovereignty was, in practice, usually limited. For example, the privatized railways had been broken-up into a plethora of regional train operators, but for passengers in any particular area, there was usually only one rail company they could travel with; for example, rail commuters between London and Bristol were mainly reliant on First Great Western. Hence the actual degree of intra-industry competition, and thus consumer choice, was very limited in the privatized railways, and similar limitations were a feature of most other privatized industries. Such have been the serious financial and organizational problems affecting Britain's railways since privatization that the coordinating body Railtrack was taken back into public owner-ship, via Network Rail, in 2002, and several regional rail operators have also been taken over by the state or the Welsh government during the last two decades, although in England, these take-overs have usually been viewed as temporary pending a return to private ownership.

In tacit acknowledgment that privatization did not automatically result in higher quality services and lower prices for customers via competition, the Thatcher–Major governments appointed a plethora of regulatory bodies both to monitor the performance of each privatized industry, and stipulate their pricing regime, such as the permissible increase in charges that could be imposed each year. These regulatory bodies (Office of the Rail Regulator, Office of the Gas and Electricity Markets, Office of Communications, etc) were also empowered to impose fines on privatized industries that failed to achieve specified performance standards or targets. While this regulatory regime was intended to serve the interests of customers, by ensuring that poor ser-vice would result in the privatized company or sector being financially penalized, it nonetheless reflected the extent to which a genuinely com-petitive and self-regulating market was limited, or non-existent, among many privatized industries and utilities. This therefore necessitated new layers of bureaucracy to be established by ministers, albeit operating on a semi-autonomous or arms-length basis: their framework and objec-tives would be politically determined, but day-to-day operations and internal management were largely the responsibility of the regulatory bodies themselves.

Meanwhile, as also noted in Chapter 3, the public sector has, since the 1980s, been subject to intense managerialism, reflecting the Thatcherite premise that many professionals working in education, healthcare, pro-bation and social work – Thatcher would brook no criticism of the police

– were either incompetent and/or lazy, due to the lack of competition and absence of a profit motive, a supposed jobs-for-life ethos, or because they prioritized professional self-interest over the interests of their "clients". To eradicate this perceived problem, the Thatcher governments (and all their successors, including New Labour), subjected the public sector to a regime of relentless and rigorous monitoring, performance measurement and target-setting, with the expectation that efficiency, cost-effectiveness, productivity or output, and "customer satisfaction" would all improve annually. Marketization alone was deemed insufficient to galvanize public sector professionals to become more competitive, industrious and responsive to the needs and wishes of their clients.

Yet in addition to greatly increased administrative control and the imposition of strict regulatory procedures on professional staff, managerialism also entailed regular audits and inspections of public sector institutions, and these are often extremely detailed in the data and information they required – "robust" in management-speak. Consequently, many frontline professionals devote a considerable amount of time both preparing for these institutional audits, and then actually participating in them while they are being conducted, either by being observed, interviewed, or simply completing the reams of paperwork or online box-ticking involved. Some public sector professionals lament that their careers have become an endless cycle of audits, and that preparing for the next institutional inspection is ascribed almost as much importance as the day-to-day professional activities supposedly being measured.

To compound the frustration that many public sector professionals experience under this hyper-managerialist regime, they are often obliged to perform their professional roles in a manner which renders them bureaucratically or statistically measurable. Hence this audit culture does not simply measure individual or institutional performance in the public sector, it determines *what* is worth measuring, and *how* it can or should be measured. This frequently reduces professional tasks to a tick-box formula, which, in turn, enables the data to be published in league tables, or other user-friendly visual format in the name of "transparency".

However, this yielded another paradox of Thatcherism and its legacy, namely that the public sector has become characterized by excessive bureaucracy and red tape, due to the hyper-managerialist emphasis on regulating and measuring the activities and performance of doctors, nurses, probation officers, social workers, teachers and university lecturers, according to criteria such as cost-effectiveness, efficiency, output and value-added (Travers 2007). Not only has the public sector witnessed an enormous increase in the number and authority of managers and senior administrators – business managers, human resources staff, corporate compliance officers, quality assurance officers, and strategic coordinators – in each sphere or institution, there has also been a vastly increased emphasis on rigorous and quantifiable procedures and processes.

Professionals are not only expected to achieve more in terms of specified results and targets ("key performance indicators" in corporate jargon), but increasingly compelled to perform their roles and duties in a specified and quantifiable manner by following clear and strict administrative routines. As a consequence, the ability to exercise professional discretion, expertise and judgement when making decisions has been steadily eroded, and increasingly subordinated to bureaucratic criteria and regulatory requirements imposed from above, often stipulated by people who have little, if any, experience of performing the task(s) they are managing and measuring.

Herein lie further contradictions and paradoxes of Thatcherism and its legacy in the public sector. First, although Thatcherites berate the baleful effect of bureaucracy on the private sector, which cannot thrive if it is tied-up in red tape, it is assumed that the public sector will only become more efficient and provide an improved service if it is subject to regular and robust bureaucratic monitoring, regulatory diktats, and routine surveillance. The red tape which apparently suffocates and stifles the private sector is somehow meant to stimulate and spur the public sector.

The second paradox, directly following on from this, is that having originally berated the public sector for its bloated bureaucracy and concomitant inefficiency, Thatcherite reform of the public sector (which has continued unabated since the end of her premiership) has itself spawned a sprawling and stifling bureaucracy, entailing seemingly impenetrable layers of middle managers and senior administrators, to micro-manage and relentlessly monitor frontline or public-facing professionals.

A perverse consequence of this hyper-managerialist regime is that public service professionals are constantly distracted or prevented from serving their clients or the public, efficiently and enthusiastically, due to the onerous and time-consuming administrative demands placed upon them in the name of accountability and performance evaluation. In 2018, a nurse confessed that "I am not sure if I want to stay in nursing, I feel the care I give is compromised by trying to complete specific tasks which are more concerned with audit and performance rather than care of the patient" (quoted in Matthews-King 2018). Similar complaints about bureaucracy and paperwork are commonplace among teachers too, with one teacher, in 2022, confessing that "I am desperate to get out of education due to workload, constant monitoring and paperwork" (quoted in *The Guardian* 2022a). Meanwhile, in 2016, the leader of the Association of Teachers and Lecturers, Mary Bousted, complained that "so much of what they [teachers] are doing isn't related to effective teaching and learning. It's just bureaucratic paper filling, data driven, mind-numbingly useless work", which is being done "for accountability purposes rather than raising standards of teaching and learning" (BBC News online 2016).

The police too have become burdened by bureaucracy and red tape, and regularly complain that the volume of paperwork and form-filling impedes their ability to tackle crime, although presumably in some court cases, a prosecution fails or a defendant is acquitted because the police officers did not follow the correct procedure (Hymas 2019). The police have also complained that the pressure to hit bureaucratic or quantitative targets means that they are sometimes obliged to ignore more serious or complex crimes that would take longer to investigate and solve, and instead focus on minor or victimless crimes which enable a quick arrest and prosecution, and therefore improve statistics for convictions. This would be an example of the audit culture prioritizing quantitative over qualitative criteria in conducting performance measurements.

The final tragedy or insult for public sector professionals is that these problems are then cited by Thatcherite Conservatives and Britain's predominantly right-wing press as evidence of the ingrained inefficiency of the public sector, and the incurable laziness or incompetence of many of its staff, whereupon yet more reforms are proposed, to extend marketization and intensify managerialism even further. The public sector is then lectured about the need to modernize, embrace change, and get out of its comfort zone, as if it had been completely left alone and unreformed for the past 40 years, when so many of the problems and dysfunctionalities in education, healthcare, policing, the probation service and social work, are a direct and entirely predictable consequence of these reforms. Yet as Ian Gilmour noted: "People in the grip of dogma ... possessed by ideology and delusion ... are neither susceptible to reason nor prone to the admission of error" (Gilmour 1992: 32).

Britain's housing crisis

As we noted in Chapter 3, the right-to-buy policy of selling council houses became one of the flagship policies of the Thatcher governments during the 1980s, and was part of a wider commitment to private-ownership of property intrinsic to neoliberalism and its innate acquisitive individualism. However, in insisting that local authorities should *not* build new homes to replace those which had been sold to their tenants, Thatcherism partly precipitated the housing crisis that Britain, and young people especially, are confronted with today. This is another policy that has become embedded, as successive governments since Thatcher's premiership have largely continued with her unequivocal preference for private sector or individualized housing provision via homeownership and renting from landlords, and the marketization of housing associations whose tenants are often socio-economically disadvantaged, but are now expected to pay market rents.

In the context of population growth, and demographic trends like more divorce (invariably necessitating two properties rather than the one that the couple previously lived in) and people generally living longer, the failure or refusal of successive governments since the 1980s to commit to a programme of building low-cost or affordable homes, and social housing, has meant that property prices and rents have increased inexorably. In accordance with the immutable laws of the market, the demand for housing has consistently exceeded the supply, resulting in escalating house prices, rents that sometimes consume more than half of a person's take-home pay (and which precludes them from saving-up the 10 per cent deposit typically required to obtain a mortgage), more people in house-shares well into their late 20s and 30s, and a growing number of young people financially compelled to move back to the parental home after university.

This has wider or longer-term societal consequences, such as many young people postponing, or even abandoning altogether, plans to start a family of their own, because they simply cannot afford to buy a 2–3 bedroom house; whereas 30–40 years ago, such a property would have cost about three or four times the average salary, it is now likely to cost eight to ten times more than what many people earn annually. Given that higher house prices also necessitate a larger deposit – 10 per cent of £250,000 evidently being much more than 10 per cent of £60,000 – it is clear that for many young people today, homeownership is not affordable, unless they either have relatively wealthy parents, or they can access one of the relatively new shared-ownership properties that are becoming available, whereby a percentage of the property's value is purchased with a mortgage, and the remainder is rented. If the tenant subsequently becomes financially better-off, or perhaps meets a long-term partner with whom they can pool their incomes, they can then increase their mortgaged share of the property, and reduce the amount of rent they pay accordingly.

Yet it is commonly believed, as reported via public surveys and opinion polls, that the main reason why many young people are unable to afford to become homeowners is not because of high house prices, exorbitant rents, and more than a decade of stagnant salaries, but because they spend too much money on streaming services and on lattes in high-street cafes (*Guardian* 2022b). On this basis, a young person cancelling their £10.99 monthly Netflix subscription would be able to save £131.88 per year, such that in 189 years, they could have saved enough to pay the 10 per cent deposit on a £250,000 property!

Meanwhile, many picturesque rural villages, or coastal towns, especially in Cornwall, have seen young people priced-out, and effectively compelled to move away, due to wealthy city-dwellers buying holiday homes or second homes used for occasional weekend breaks. With the younger population moving away, due to the lack of secure or well-paid jobs (many jobs in Cornish coastal communities are seasonal, coinciding with summer tourism) *and* the lack of affordable housing, the community becomes characterized by a growing number of properties that are empty during the week, or even most of the year. In turn, local shops and amenities become unprofitable and cease trading, whereupon these previously vibrant and close-knit communities become "ghost" villages and towns inhabited mainly by the elderly, and as they pass away, local customs and traditions die with them.

Moreover, their home is likely to be added to the portfolio of a buy-to-let landlord or "second homer", thereby compounding the local housing shortage and further fuelling the exodus of young people. For example, there are more than 7,000 empty homes in Cornwall, due their official owners living and working elsewhere, while in the UK over-all, there are over 200,000 residential properties which are empty on a long-term basis (for more than six months). Not surprisingly, perhaps, there is now a growing backlash against second-homers, holiday lets or Airbnbs, as local residents in some affected towns are attempting to "take back control" of their communities (Drury 2022; Ellson 2022; Hotchin 2022; York 2022a).

In recent years, house-builders have been formally required to ensure that a proportion of new homes are "affordable", but this stipulation has been subject both to pressure from Conservative neoliberals who view it as political interference in the market and red tape imposed on the construction industry, and some property companies, with a few of the latter seeking legal loopholes to avoid the formal requirement. Since 2020, some ministers have considered relaxing the requirement, so that the statutory obligation to provide a percentage of affordable homes would only apply to developments involving a larger number of prop-erties; perhaps 40 or 50, rather than just 10 (*The Times* 2022).

The dysfunctional housing market bequeathed by Thatcherism and its entrenched neoliberalism has yielded one further, increasingly seri-ous, problem, namely the inability of some companies or public-sector organizations to recruit enough staff because potential applicants or employees would not be able to afford to rent or buy if they relocated. This problem is particularly prevalent in and around London, of course, where most property prices and rents greatly exceed average salaries, and thus inhibit labour mobility (Webber 2018). It also strongly affects younger workers, because they naturally start on lower salaries than older or more experienced staff (Judge 2019). Even the additional London weighting is not usually sufficient to ameliorate this problem. For example, some hospitals in London are now struggling to fill nurs-ing vacancies, because many nurses cannot afford the cost of renting a flat in the city (York 2022b).

The high rents that many people must pay if they cannot afford to buy a property has also caused problems for the Conservatives' commitment to reducing welfare spending and "dependency", because many tenants have been/are eligible to claim Housing Benefit, which is a means-tested social security benefit paid to people with low incomes and high rents.

Despite periodic attempts to reduce the amounts that individuals can claim – perhaps by expecting them to move to cheaper accommodation, or even a different part of the country where housing costs are lower – the total amount paid in Housing Benefit in 2014–15 was £23.4 billion, but declined thereafter, so that in 2020–21, it was £17.2 billion. This is another consequence of the political failure or refusal to build more/enough local authority and/or affordable housing and compelling housing associations to charge market-based rents. Moreover, these payments mean that, in effect, billions of tax-payers' money is being paid to private landlords each year, yet they are rarely mentioned when Conservatives and the press denounce welfare dependency, the abuse of the social security system, or people receiving public funds that they do not really need.

Ultimately, therefore, high rents and property prices are having a damaging effect on local communities, would-be families, the labour market, and the welfare state, yet there remains an ideological reluctance or refusal to revive or expand social or public housing, and instead, a continued insistence on private provision via traditional homeownership, further reliance on private rentals, and advocacy of further deregulation of the housing market to encourage more landlords. In spite of evidence to the contrary during the past 30 years, Thatcherites still assume that greater competition between (more) landlords will result in lower rents for tenants, as landlords compete against each other to fill their vacant properties or rooms.

The socially destabilizing consequences of Thatcherism

More generally, several commentators – from a variety of ideological perspectives, including Conservatives themselves, or commentators who initially lauded some aspects or objectives of Thatcherism – have subsequently lamented the extent to which the Thatcherite promotion of relentless competition, change/modernization and acquisitive individualism has fatally destroyed cohesion, continuity, community, reciprocal duties and social stability. Or as Marx observed, under unfettered capitalism, "All that is solid melts into air. All that is sacred is profaned" in the relentless pursuit of profit and short-term economic benefits or financial gain. Again, some of these consequences have only become fully evident in the decades after the Thatcher premiership, but they nonetheless derive from the practical consequences of Thatcherite economic policies, the fetishization of the market, the recasting of citizens into consumers, and the intensification of corporate competition and labour market flexibility. As one commentator notes: "One of her hopes was that she would create a more moral society ... yet the materialistic and self-centred 1980s culture that her liberal economic policies often encouraged was the antithesis of her aims" (Seldon 2021: 132).

One of the most trenchant critiques of Thatcherism's negative impact on social continuity, stability and tradition, emanates from the political theorist, John Gray, who portrays Thatcherite neoliberalism, and its veneration of the market, as profoundly unconservative in many of its consequences and impacts. In accusing Thatcherism of heralding "the undoing of Conservatism" he laments that "inherited institutions and practices have been swept away by the market forces which Neoliberal forces release or reinforce", and as such, many "contemporary conservatives have ... abandoned any claim to be guardians of continuity in national life". Gray argues that "unconstrained market institutions are bound to undermine social and political stability, particularly as they impose on the population unprecedented levels of economic insecurity with all the resultant dislocations of life in families and communities", adding that "market forces – especially when they are global – work to unsettle communities and delegitimate traditional institutions". As these market forces have been entrenched and expanded since the 1980s, they have "worked to extend to the middle classes the insecurities and risks that have always plagued working-class life" (Gray 1994: 7, 9, 10).

Moreover, Gray laments the manner in which "the mobility of labour required ... in a society dominated by unconstrained market institutions, is profoundly disruptive of settled communities and imposes severe strains on life in families", while also promoting "a cult of mobility that consort badly with the settled communities cherished by traditional conservatives". Ultimately, the practical consequence of "market liberalism is ... ineluctably destructive of tradition and community", and "inimical to the values that traditional conservatives hold dear". In a society dominated by unrestrained individualism and neoliberalism, and in thrall to the inviolable and insatiable needs of the market: "Status is ephemeral, trust frail, and contract sovereign" (Gray 1994: 19, 20, 22).

Needless to say, the relationship between employers and employees, companies and their staff, becomes merely transactional: corporations and managers no longer have any moral obligation to the welfare of their staff, or wider social responsibility. Their only objectives are to maximize annual profits and shareholder value, and if that entails making hundreds or thousands of loyal, hard-working, employees redundant in order to reduce labour costs and the salaries bill, then so be it. In turn, workers learn that they are entirely expendable and only a pay cheque or two away from dismissal and/or unemployment, and so any notion of loyalty to "their" company or employer dissipates. In a wider sense, the erstwhile conservative vision of a stable organic society which enshrines mutual ties and reciprocal responsibilities is further undermined, and individuals are left defenceless against, and subservient to, untrammelled market forces and huge, impersonal, corporations.

In 1993, the then Conservative prime minister, John Major (borrowing from George Orwell), speculated that in 50 years' time Britain would still be characterized by "long shadows on county (cricket) grounds, warm beer, green suburbs, dog lovers, and old maids cycling to holy communion through the morning mist". However, some of Major's bucolic vision was becoming redundant even as he spoke, and much more of it has certainly been undermined subsequently by the rampant neoliberalism and commercialization bequeathed by Thatcherism – which Major and his governments did nothing to reject or reverse. Formerly languid five-day cricket matches are increasingly being superseded by T20 contests in which two sides bat for 20 overs, meaning that the game lasts for a matter of hours, not days. More recently, The Hundred has been introduced, whereby "franchise" teams (such as Northern Superchargers, and Trent Rockets) face 100 balls in a single-innings match. Needless to say, the introduction of these new, short-game, cricketing formats is largely driven by commercial imperatives.

Elsewhere, it has become slightly more difficult to buy a pint of "warm beer" because there are fewer pubs in Britain today: the number of pubs in the UK has declined from 64,000 in 1990 (when Major became prime minister) to 47,000 in 2022. Many of these former pubs have been sold to property developers to be transformed into apartments. Meanwhile, the so-called old maids having cycled to church, would find it sparsely attended, partly because of secularization, but also because for many people, Sunday is merely another day of the week, rather than a holy day, or simply a day of rest. Indeed, many people, especially in the retail and service sectors, now are obliged to work on Sundays, in accordance with the Thatcherite veneration of consumerism and "labour market flexibility". Shopping centres and out-of-town superstores are our new cathedrals.

In effect, the relentless pursuit of Thatcherism has destroyed much of Conservatism, in terms of continuity, defence of established institutions, incrementalism, mutual respect and reciprocal obligations, organic society, respect for custom and practice, reverence for accumulated or inherited wisdom, social stability and traditional communities. Indeed, one non-Thatcherite Conservative has claimed that far from mellowing with age and time, Thatcher became "even more stridently right-wing", such that despite saving Britain from rampant inflation, excessive taxation and trade union power, "she paradoxically also came close to destroying the Conservative Party" (Patten 2018: 151). Moreover, while in the 1980s Thatcherism wreaked havoc on much of the working class, in terms of the decimation of traditional industries and the concomitant hollowing-out and impoverishment of previously close-knit communities, which had been based around the local coalmine, shipyard or textile mill, since the 1990s the continued implementation of Thatcherite policies has increasingly destabilized the middle class.

A growing number of white-collar workers and professionals have increasingly been affected by unwelcome economic and employment changes, as the drive for increased (and quicker) profitability and shareholder value has exposed many middle-class jobs to automation, contracting-out, longer or unsocial working-hours (the decline of 9–5 Monday–Friday as the norm), more intense working practices, sundry performance indicators, and regular redundancies in the guise of corporate restructuring and cost-cutting, as well regular assaults on allegedly unaffordable occupational pensions. As Chris Patten laments, Thatcher "came close not only to wrecking the Conservative Party but also, in the longer term, to corroding the middle-class values" which she professed to venerate and seemingly personified (Patten 2018: 143).

Indeed, in some respects, various aspects of Thatcherism came to bear some remarkable similarities with the Soviet Marxism it despised – a supposedly infallible ideology, extrapolated from hallowed texts and theories, which only heretics or subversives wilfully failed or refused to support. The supposed intellectual and logical coherence and consistency of the ideology – as interpreted and decreed by its acolytes – meant that any problems were ascribed either to failures in implementing it with sufficient rigour and vigour, or to deliberate attempts at subversion and sabotage by enemies within (often the individuals and institutions mentioned above). In such circumstances, its proponents repeatedly assumed that their ideology either needed to be applied with even more energy and enthusiasm, regardless of the material hardship and misery this inflicted on many citizens, or the alleged saboteurs and subversives needed to be identified, denounced, and/or removed from their posts altogether.

What Thatcherites – just like other ideologues – were/are never willing to contemplate when faced with practical problems or unintended consequences was that the ideology itself might be inherently flawed; that its theoretical assumptions, philosophical logic, or inherent laws might themselves be erroneous, and thus doomed to fail. That the principles and precepts on which a political doctrine is based could be incorrect or invalid is something which ideologues lack the humility to accept, and so they repeatedly look for explanations and reasons beyond their ideology to explain failures to achieve specified policy goals or the intended socio-economic transformation.

Consequently, any crisis is assumed to necessitate a doubling-down in the application and implementation of the ideology on which the regime is based, accompanied both by parallel reforms to render the relevant institutions more effective (compliant), and a new witch-hunt to identify – or manufacture – the enemies within who are accused of sabotaging the expected success of the ideology and its policies.

Concluding comments

Thatcherism has proved to be a controversial, divisive, often contradictory, yet enduring, feature of British politics since the late 1980s, with its legacy and consequences still highly visible today; indeed, perhaps more evident than ever before. To her adherents and admirers, the ideas and policies that constituted Thatcherism, and which were (and still are) faithfully promoted by many of Britain's most widely read daily newspapers, delivered national salvation for a Britain that had experienced economic decline, moral decay and social disorder since the 1960s. Thatcherites would point proudly to achievements, such as lower taxation; wider share ownership; increased homeownership; greatly enhanced individual liberty; much more consumer choice and sovereignty; reduced inflation and the restoration of sound money; curbs on welfare dependency; fewer strikes by trade unions; the ability of individuals to become financially better-off via hard work and entrepreneurship; the breaking-up of inefficient and expensive monopolies in industry, the public sector and local government; a cutting of bureaucracy and red tape; a general "rolling back" of the state to set people free, and allow them to decide for themselves how and where to spend their hard-earned money.

Against this positive interpretation, the critics of Thatcherism would argue that: inequality and poverty have increased exponentially since the 1980s, such that Britain is now characterized by an enormous chasm between the rich and the poor, with many working people reliant on top-up welfare benefits and/or food banks due to poverty wages; for many ordinary people on average incomes, overall taxation has not been reduced, because their income tax cuts were offset (and partly funded) by increases in national insurance and VAT; the deliberate refusal to build social housing has bequeathed today's chronic lack of affordable housing and high private sector rents; labour market flexibility has resulted in worsening terms and conditions of employment, negligible workers' rights and employment protection, and many workers suffering from debilitating stress or other mental health problems due to increased pressure and performance monitoring in the work place, as well as growing job insecurity and precarity; what is sometimes termed the "gig economy" and a race to the bottom or levelling-down in terms of deteriorating employment conditions and declining pay, even for sections of the middle class.

That Thatcherism yielded such diverse and irreconcilable perspectives is itself a reflection of its eclectic and often contradictory character (as noted in the previous chapter), and the uneven impact of its policies: some sections of British society prospered, while others effectively perished. As some individuals amassed enormous wealth, others sank into socio-economic deprivation, bequeathing a Britain which today is characterized by extreme inequality, and in which the CEOs of some of Britain's largest companies are paid at least 100 times more than their shopfloor or customer-facing staff. Supporters of Thatcherism could point to the wide range of new white-collar and service sector jobs created, and opportunities thereupon offered, as a combined consequence of entrepreneurship, deregulation, tax cuts and the trickle-down of wealth. Critics would point to the decimation of industries, jobs and communities in much of northern England and south Wales, which neither benefited from the new sources of employment mostly located in London and the South-east, nor from the much-vaunted trickle-down of wealth; the flow of which dries-up in the home counties.

The eclectic character of Thatcherism is also a major reason for its electoral appeal and popularity among different sections of British society in the 1980s (and beyond). Some supporters were attracted by the commitment to liberalize and deregulate the economy by "rolling back the state", cutting taxes and restoring individual liberty. This supposedly enhanced freedom by offering people opportunities to start their own businesses and/or keep more of the money they earned, and also by promoting consumerism whereby individuals could choose how and where they spent their money, rather than having the state spend it on their behalf on supposedly free public services. This aspect of Thatcherism was particularly attractive to sections of the petite bourgeoisie, small businesses, the self-employed, and sections of the aspirational working class that wanted to emulate or join the middle class via greater prosperity, homeownership and starting their own business.

On the other hand, some of the support for Thatcher(ism) derived from authoritarianism and a deeply conservative stance on moral and social issues pertaining to non-traditional lifestyles, crime, immigration and sexual politics. This source of support for Thatcherism was concerned that, in many respects, there had been too much freedom and liberty – for other people, of course, or the "wrong" sort of people – in Britain since the 1960s, and that the urgent need was for the state to be rolled forwards, and governmental authority reimposed, along with traditional morality or "Victorian values". This socially conservative stance was (and remains) very popular among sections of the English provincial middle class – which has long viewed itself as the economic and moral backbone of the nation – but it also proved attractive to a strand of working-class authoritarianism that is disdainful of minorities or other sections of society that it strongly dislikes or disapproves of, due to their seemingly alternative lifestyles or sexuality: it needs to be borne in mind that Britain was very much more homophobic and openly racist in the 1970s and 1980s, thus providing political opportunities for the populist right (on the characteristics and causes of working-class authoritarianism, see Lipset 1959; 1960: ch. 4).

Thatcher herself successfully appealed to such moral absolutism, social conservatism and authoritarianism via her rhetorical and populist discourse, which reflected and reinforced a sense of political crises and national vulnerability through the construction of binary opposites (Charteris-Black 2005: ch. 4; Dorey 2015; Heppell, Crines & Dorey 2016). Through this discursive technique, she presented her audiences with a series of either/or, good/bad, alternatives. This also sometimes entailed drawing distinction between virtuous majorities and subversive or unpopular minorities. Needless to say, she and the Conservatives were depicted as being aligned with the former, while Labour and the left were ascribed to the latter, such as hard-working people vs welfare scroungers, consumer sovereignty vs producer interests, trade union moderates vs trade union militants, and law-abiding majority vs criminals, for example.

In a 1984 speech, Thatcher was more explicit in depicting a clear choice between Labour's policies (bad) and the Conservatives' (good):

> On high-spending councils, Labour supports the town hall bosses. We stand up for the ratepayers.
>
> On de-nationalisation, Labour defends state monopoly. We stand up for the customers.
>
> On trade union reform, Labour sides with the trade union bosses. We stand up for the members.
>
> On council house sales, Labour loves to be the landlord. We stand up for the tenants.
>
> On taxes, Labour wants more of your money. We stand up for the taxpayers.
>
> (TF 1984e)

Two years later, in her conference speech, Thatcher invoked the rhetorical device of *parison* to ascribe a series of negative policy attributes and objectives to the Labour Party:

> What the Labour Party of today wants is:
> Housing – municipalised;
> Industry – nationalised;
> The police service – politicised;
> The judiciary – radicalised;
> Union membership – tyrannised;
> And above all – and most serious of all – our defences neutralised
> (TF 1986b)

In rhetorically presenting the British people with a binary choice between good/evil (Conservatism/socialism), she sometimes incorporated religious symbolism and biblical references into her speeches and other public statements. For example, in a televized interview with Dr Miriam Stoppard, Thatcher insisted that "we have a choice … between good and evil. Every person has it" (TF 1985b). She reiterated this perspective in a speech to the General Assembly of the Church of Scotland, declaring "from the beginning man has been endowed by God with the fundamental right to choose between good and evil" (TF 1988b). A decade earlier, in 1978, Thatcher had warned that: "The Devil is still with us, recording his successes in the crime figures and in all the other maladies of this society", adding that: "As a Christian, I am bound to shun Utopias on this earth" (TF 1978i).

Furthermore, Thatcher often characterized her political views and values as constituting a crusade or a faith, thereby further imbuing them with a religious dimension. For example, she informed the Conservative Party's 1976 conference that they were henceforth embarking on "a crusade not merely to put a temporary brake on socialism, but to stop its forward march once and for all" (TF 1976b). Then, in 1986, when extolling her government's privatization policy, in a speech at the annual Lord Mayor's banquet, Thatcher declared that "Popular capitalism is a crusade: a crusade to enfranchise the many in the economic life of Britain" (TF 1986a).

Elsewhere, in a speech during the 1979 election campaign, Thatcher claimed that: "The Old Testament prophets didn't go out into the highways saying, 'Brothers, I want consensus'. They said, 'This is my faith and my vision! This is what I passionately believe!' And they preached it. We have a message. Go out, preach it, practice it, fight for it – and the day will be ours!" (TF 1979a). A few months later she informed delegates at the 1979 party conference that having "kept faith" during the recent period in opposition, "you will, I know, keep faith through the far longer years of Conservative government that are to come" (TF 1979b).

Moreover, by invoking such biblical and religious analogies and metaphors, Thatcher sought to suggest that Britain itself was engaged in a battle for spiritual, as much as political, salvation, which only she and her mode of Conservatism could deliver: "The very survival of our laws, our institutions, our national character – that is what is at stake today' (1976 conference). Thatcher thus viewed and depicted British politics as a Manichean battle between Conservatism and socialism, between liberty and state control, between democracy and dictatorship, between wealth creation and poverty, and between a free-market economy and a Soviet-style centralized command economy. By 1980, however, Thatcher was proudly declaring that "We are winning the battle of ideas', albeit insisting that: "It is essential for us to continue winning this battle" (Thatcher 1980).

Meanwhile, because Thatcher and her acolytes were engaged in an explicit battle against the philosophy and policies that had prevailed in Britain since 1945, and which therefore rendered Thatcherism unmistakably and unashamedly ideological, it constituted a clear divergence or departure from traditional Conservatism, given the latter's emphasis on accumulated wisdom, continuity, defence of established institutions, incrementalism, moderation, organicism, reciprocal roles and responsibility between constituent classes, social harmony and stability (as far as practicably possible), and the rejection of abstract ideas and theories as the basis of radical political reform or reconstruction.

However, ideologically or philosophically, Thatcherism did share significant similarities with the category of "combative Conservatism" identified by Norton and Aughey. Whereas "progressive Toryism" aims to adapt Conservatism to seemingly ineluctable change and sees itself as forward-thinking or enlightened, and "pessimistic Toryism" laments change and so-called progress but feels that it is mostly inevitable, such that Conservatives should aim to limit or ameliorate the negative consequences and associated instability, "combative Toryism" not only resents change when it results in more state intervention in the economy and an apparent drift toward socialism, it insists that Conservatives can – and should – resist and reverse this trajectory (Norton & Aughey 1981: 75–9, 68–72). As Norton and Aughey explain:

> Combative Toryism exhorts Conservatives not to be ashamed of, or defensive about, their prejudices and beliefs, but to popularize them. Combative Toryism is Conservative instinct made articulate, and these instincts and values are held to be more in tune with the real needs and desires of the electorate than the utopian dreams of Socialism. It indulges in a populist appeal that expresses itself in a blunt and earthy fashion. Its targets are the faceless bureaucracy of central and local government, and the misguided do-gooders of no practical wisdom. (Norton & Aughey 1981: 82)

More specifically, the "combative Tory" is adamant that wealth should accrue from individual effort, governments should only provide social support for those in most genuine and unavoidable need, the traditional family and the rule of law are the basis of a free society, and the principles and practices of hard work, enterprise, property ownership, self-advancement and thrift should be venerated.

The combative mode of Conservatism represented by Thatcherism, and Thatcher's own professed pursuit of "conviction politics", meant that the Conservative Party since the 1980s has largely ceased to be conservative, beyond the objective of providing an "intellectual justification of inequalities in society, and the preservation of the privileges that such inequalities entail", this being "the essence of the Conservative Party's role ... to formulate policy that conserves a hierarchy of wealth and power" while persuading the masses that this is reasonable, and that they themselves benefit from such inequality (Norton & Aughey 1981: 47).

Apart from vehemently defending inequality and, indeed, arguing that there needed to be more of it to reverse the post-1945 "obsession" with egalitarianism, fairness and social justice, Thatcherism was often very unconservative in its ideological character and lack of respect for established institutions, especially when these were viewed as inimical to the promotion of free-market economics and an enterprise culture. This disdain for intermediary institutions has continued since Thatcher's premiership; indeed, has intensified under the premierships of Boris Johnson and Liz Truss. For more mainstream or moderate Conservatives, this has been a serious source of concern, with one of Theresa May's former senior aides, Gavin Barwell (2022) emphasizing the importance of "strong institutions ... rule of law, Unionism, sound money: these are some of the pillars on which the Conservative party is built". However, he lamented that: "The Johnson and Truss governments have weakened some of those institutions ... It is shocking to see the party's leaders so casually undermine them". Similarly concerned was Robert Halfron, who, just a few weeks into Liz Truss's premiership, complained that: "The impression the new government has given is that it is run by libertarian jihadists, blowing up the Conservative Party and the country in the process" (Halfron 2022).

One of the legacies of Thatcherism, and the concomitant fetishization of the free market, is that the Conservative Party has become increasingly ideological, and as such, repeatedly assumes that any economic or social problems are *not* due to any inherent deficiencies or discrepancies within the ideology itself, but a failure to enact and implement the ideology with sufficient purity and perseverance, due either to insufficient faith or commitment among key individuals, or because governing institutions are proving to be an obstructive impediment, in which case they need to be reformed, removed or replaced. Thatcherism has destroyed much of Conservatism.

Chronology

1925   Margaret Hilda Roberts born in Grantham.

1959   Elected as Member of Parliament for Finchley.

1970   Appointed Secretary of State for Education and Science by Edward Heath.

1974   Conservatives lose February and October general elections. Thatcher establishes Centre for Policy Studies with Sir Keith Joseph and Alfred Sherman.

1975   Conservative MPs elect Margaret Thatcher as Conservative leader.

1978–79   "Winter of discontent"

1979   Conservatives win general election in May. Chancellor Geoffrey Howe cuts top rate of income tax from 83 per cent to 60 per cent, but increases VAT from 8 per cent to 15 per cent.

1980   The "right-to-buy" policy allows council house tenants to buy their home, with discounts on the purchase price offered according to length of tenancy. First law enacted to curb trade unions.

1981   Thatcher's first cabinet reshuffle sees some key "wets" sacked or moved to less prestigious posts.

1982   Argentina invades the Falkland Islands. British army and Royal Navy liberate them, and restore the Falklands to self-government under British sovereignty. Thatcher's popularity soars against a backdrop of patriotic pride. Second law enacted to curb trade unions.

1983   Conservatives win a landslide 144-seat parliamentary majority, while Labour slumps to 27 per cent share of votes cast.

1984   The IRA detonate a bomb in the Brighton Hotel in an attempt to assassinate Thatcher where many senior Conservatives and their spouses are staying for the Conservative Party annual conference. One Conservative MP is killed, as is the wife of John Wakeham, a cabinet minister. The wife of another cabinet minister, Norman Tebbit, is paralysed, and requires 24/7 care for the rest of her life. British Telecom privatized with some shares sold directly to the public. Third law enacted to curb trade unions. National Union of Mineworkers, led by Arthur Scargill, embark upon a year-long strike in opposition to anticipated closure of "uneconomic" mines and widespread redundancies. Thatcher Government stands firm and the strike crumbles 12 months later.

1986   British Gas privatized, with some shares again sold directly to the public. "Big Bang" deregulation of financial services and banks. Greater London Council and 6 metropolitan councils (all Labour-controlled) abolished.

1987   Conservatives win another landslide general election victory. British Airways and Rolls Royce privatized.

1988   Top rate of income tax educed from 60 per cent to 40 per cent, and the basic rate from 30 per cent to 25 per cent. British Steel privatized. Fourth law enacted to curb trade unions. Margaret Thatcher delivers her speech in Bruges.

1989   Water industry privatized. Geoffrey Howe is demoted as foreign secretary to become Leader of the House of Commons and also becomes deputy prime minister. Chancellor Nigel Lawson resigns due to policy disagreements with Thatcher and her high-profile economic adviser Alan Walters. Sir Anthony Meyer instigates a "stalking horse" leadership challenge to Thatcher. She is comfortably re-elected, but 60 Conservative MPs voted against her or abstained.

1990   Electricity industry privatized. Fifth law enacted to curb trade unions. The Community Charge (Poll Tax) introduced in England and Wales, having been introduced in Scotland the previous year. It provokes a series of riots. Nicholas Ridley resigns from the cabinet after claiming, in *The Spectator*, that the European Community was a vehicle for German domination of Western Europe. Geoffrey Howe resigns, in November, due to continued disagreement with Thatcher over policy towards the European Community. In his powerful parliamentary resignation speech, he urges someone to challenge her for the Conservative leadership. Michael Heseltine announces his candidature for the Conservative leadership, and although Thatcher wins more votes in the first ballot, she is slightly short of the 15 per cent majority the Party's rules require to win outright. Thatcher resigns before the second ballot. John Major is elected Conservative Party leader, having been endorsed by Thatcher in clear preference to either Heseltine or Douglas Hurd.

1992   John Major's Conservative government re-elected with a 21-seat majority.

1993   Thatcher delivers a speech in the House of Lords voicing her opposition to the Maastricht Treaty establishing the European Union, and expresses support for a referendum of the British people prior to ratification. Sixth law enacted to curb trade unions.

1994   Coal industry privatized. Tony Blair elected as leader of the Labour Party.

1995   Blair rewrites Clause IV of Labour's constitution, so that nationalization is no longer a goal of the Party. Thatcher subsequently declares that New Labour is her greatest achievement, because the Labour Party has been forced to accept capitalism and its free-market economy.

1996   Railways privatized.

1997   Thatcher endorses William Hague to succeed John Major as Conservative leader, rather than the pro-European Kenneth Clarke.

2001   Thatcher strongly endorses Iain Duncan Smith against Kenneth Clarke for the Conservative Party leadership, following Hague's resignation.

2004   Thatcher strongly endorses the leadership of Michael Howard, who had been elected unopposed as Conservative leader the previous year.

2010   David Cameron becomes Conservative prime minister, albeit as head of a coalition with the Liberal Democrats. In spite of previously urging the Conservatives to move on from Thatcherism, his government presides over an austerity programme that seems to signify an enthusiastic continuation of, or reversion to, Thatcherism.

2013   Margaret Thatcher dies.

2016   Referendum on continued EU membership sees 52 per cent of the UK voters opt to Leave and 48 per cent to remain. David Cameron resigns, and is succeeded as Conservative leader and prime minister by Theresa May.

2019   Unable to secure parliamentary approval – due mainly to opposition from supporters of a "hard Brexit" on the Conservative right – for her EU Withdrawal Agreement, May resigns, and is succeeded by Boris Johnson.

2022   Boris Johnson resigns, having been implicated in several scandals, and with over 50 ministers and other senior Conservatives resigning on 5–7 July. Liz Truss is elected Conservative leader in September, having based her policy pledges on Thatcher. After just 44 days as prime minister, Liz Truss resigns. Truss is replaced by the candidate she defeated just 6 weeks earlier, Rishi Sunak, who warns of imminent cuts in public expenditure.

References

Primary sources

Hansard 1975. *House of Commons Debates*, 5th series, 22 January.
Hansard 1976. *House of Commons Debates*, 5th series, 11 October.
Hansard 1981. *House of Commons Debates*, 5th series, 10 March.
Hansard 1985. *House of Commons Debates*, 6th series, 26 March.
Hansard 1990. *House of Commons Debates*, 6th series, 13 November.
National Archives (NA) 1979a. PREM 19/70, James Prior to Margaret Thatcher, 21 September.
NA 1979b. PREM 19/53, Lord Carrington to Margaret Thatcher, 8 June.
NA 1979c. PREM 19/24, Margaret Thatcher to Tim Lankester [her economic private secretary], 25 May.
NA 1979d. PREM 19/21, Memorandum on public sector pay by the Chancellor of the Exchequer, 14 September.
NA 1979e. PREM 19/656, Lord Carrington [foreign secretary] to Margaret Thatcher, 20 September.
NA 1980a. PREM 19/261, John Hoskyns to Margaret Thatcher, 1 February.
NA 1980b. PREM 19/263, John Hoskyns to Margaret Thatcher, 24 March.
NA 1980c. PREM 19/265, John Hoskyns to Margaret Thatcher, 24 October.
NA 1980d. PREM 19/265, John Hoskyns to Margaret Thatcher, 28 November.
NA 1981. PREM 19/491, John Hoskyns to Margaret Thatcher, 3 August. NA 1982a. PREM 19/667, Robert Armstrong to Clive Whitmore [PPS to Margaret Thatcher], 12 May.
NA 1982b. PREM 19/783, Ferdinand Mount to Margaret Thatcher, 26 May.
NA 1984. PREM 19/1539, Patrick Stewart-Blacker to Margaret Thatcher, 20 July.
NA 1985. PREM19/1461, John Redwood, "The Big Bang", 18 September.
NA 1986a. PREM 19/1722, Brian Griffiths to Margaret Thatcher, 13 March.
NA 1986b. PREM 19/1722, Oliver Letwin to Margaret Thatcher, 21 February.
NA 1986c. PREM 19/1863, David Willetts to Margaret Thatcher, 24 February; A. Laurance [Department of Health] to Mark Addison [Thatcher's private secretary), 5 March.
NA 1986d. PREM19/1863, Norman Fowler to Margaret Thatcher, 10 March.
NA 1986e. PREM 19/1722, Keith Joseph to Margaret Thatcher, 10 January.
NA 1986f. PREM 19/1722, Keith Joseph to Sir Patrick Mayhew, 22 April.

NA 1988. PREM 19/2017, Robert Peirce [on behalf of foreign secretary] to Charles Powell [Margaret Thatcher's SPAD on foreign affairs], 8 September.

Sherman Papers (SP) 1976. Sherman MSS (Royal Holloway Library) Box 7, Keith Joseph to Margaret Thatcher, 6 August.

SP 1977. Sherman MSS (Royal Holloway Library) Box 3, Alfred Sherman to Keith Joseph, 28 February.

Thatcher Foundation (TF) 1974. CCOPR 509/74, Keith Joseph speech in Edgbaston, 19 October.

TF 1975a. CCOPR 184/75, Speech in Glasgow, 21 February.

TF 1975b. Speech to Conservative Party Conference, 10 October.

TF 1975c. Speech to Conservative Central Council, 15 March.

TF 1975d. Speech to West Midlands Conservatives, 31 October.

TF 1975e. Thatcher MSS 2/1/1/42A, Lawson to Thatcher, 3 October.

TF 1975f. "Let Our Children Grow Tall", Speech to the Institute of SocioEconomic Studies (New York), 15 September.

TF 1975g. IEA MSS (Hoover Institution): Box 295, Minute of meeting between Keith Joseph, Michael Ivens [Aims of Industry] & Alfred Sherman, 8 September.

TF 1976a. John Hoskyns diary entry, 26 September.

TF 1976b. Speech to Conservative Party Conference, 8 October.

TF 1977a. Speech to Greater London Young Conservatives (Iain Macleod Memorial Lecture – "Dimensions of Conservatism"), 4 July.

TF 1977b. Speech to Conservative rally at Blenheim Palace, 16 July.

TF 1977c. Thatcher MSS, shadow cabinet: minutes of 175th Meeting, 6 October.

TF 1978a. CCOPR 1308/78, Speech to Conservative Party Conference, 13 October.

TF 1978b. Thatcher MSS 2/6/1/162, shadow cabinet: minutes of 199th meeting, 17 April.

TF 1978c. Thatcher MSS 2/6/1/162, shadow cabinet: minutes of 205th meeting, 15 May.

TF 1978d. Thatcher MSS 2/6/1/163, shadow cabinet: minutes of 216th meeting, 19 July.

TF 1978e. Thatcher MSS 2/6/1/163, shadow cabinet: minutes of 218th Meeting, 31 July.

TF 1978f. Thatcher MSS 2/6/1/163, shadow cabinet: minutes of 219th meeting, 4 September.

TF 1978g. THCR 2/6/2/118, Chris Patten to Margaret Thatcher, 23 August.

TF 1978h. Speech to Conservative Trade Unionists Conference, 11 March.

TF 1978i. Speech at St Lawrence Jewry ("I BELIEVE – A speech on Christianity and Politics"), 30 March.

TF 1979a. Speech to Conservative Rally in Cardiff, 16 April.

TF 1979b. Speech to Conservative Party Conference, 12 October.

TF 1980a. THCR 2/6/2/152, Alfred Sherman to Margaret Thatcher, 24 April.

TF 1980b. CCOPR 735/80, Speech to Conservative Party Conference, 10 October.

TF 1980c. THCR 2/6/2/152, Alfred Sherman to Margaret Thatcher, 29 February.

TF 1980d. THCR 2/6/2/152, Alfred Sherman to Margaret Thatcher, 10 April.

TF 1981a. THCR 2/1/4/70, David Knox to Michael Jopling [Chief Whip], 18 September; Ian Gow to Margaret Thatcher, 24 September.

TF 1981b. Hoskyns MSS, John Hoskyns to Margaret Thatcher, 20 August.

TF 1981c. THCR2/1/4/70, William van Straubenzee to Alan Walters, 2 December; Alan Walters to Ian Gow, 3 December; Ian Gow to Alan Walters, 7 December.

TF 1981d. ALW 040/325/2, Lord Carrington to Margaret Thatcher, 14 September.

TF 1981e. ALW 040/325/10, R. T. Jackling [Ministry of Defence] to Lord Carrington, 4 September.

TF 1983. THCR 3/2/116, Margaret Thatcher to John Evans [Labour MP], 5 May.

TF 1984a. The Second Carlton Lecture ("Why democracy will last"), 26 November.

TF 1984b. THCR 2/6/3/107, Speech by Peter Walker in London on miners' strike, 16 May; Speech by Peter Walker in Oxford, 30 May; Speech by Peter Walker in London, 30 June.

TF 1984c. THCR 1/1/19, Thatcher speech to the 1922 Committee, 19 July.

TF 1984d. THCR 1/12/26, David Hart to Margaret Thatcher, 18 September.

TF 1984e. Speech to Conservative Central Council, 24 March.

TF 1985a. Speech to Scottish Conservative Party Conference, 10 May.

TF 1985b. Interview for Yorkshire Television, *Woman to Woman*, 2 October.

TF 1986a. Speech at Lord Mayor's Banquet, 10 November.

TF 1986b. Speech to Conservative Party Conference, 10 October.

TF 1987. Speech to Conservative Party Conference, 9 October.

TF 1988a. Speech to the College of Europe ("The Bruges Speech"), 20 September.

TF 1988b. Speech to General Assembly of the Church of Scotland ("The Sermon on the Mound"), 21 May.

TF 1989a. THCR 1/1/50A, Mark Lennox-Boyd to Margaret Thatcher, 8 December.

TF 1989b. Younger MSS, George Younger's "Post Mortem Meeting Notes (MT campaign team's secret discussion)", 6 December.

TF 1990a. THCR 2/6/4/56, Robin Harris to Margaret Thatcher, 16 November.

TF 1990b. THCR 2/6/4/56, No.10 briefing – "Heseltine and Labour: the Similarities", 19 November.

Secondary sources

Abromeit, H. 1988. "British privatisation policy". *Parliamentary Affairs* 41(1): 68–85.

Aitken, J. 2013. *Margaret Thatcher: Power and Personality*. London: Bloomsbury.

Alderman, R. & N. Carter 1991. "A very Tory coup: the ousting of Mrs Thatcher". *Parliamentary Affairs* 44(2): 125–39.

Bacon, R. & W. Eltis 1976. *Britain's Economic Problem: Too Few Producers*. London: Macmillan.

Baker, K. 1993. *The Turbulent Years*. London: Faber.

Baker, P. 2022. *Outrageous! The Story of Section 28 and Britain's Battle for LGBT Education*. London: Reaktion.

Baldry, T. 1985. "Time to talk". *Reformer* [The Tory Reform Group journal], Summer.

Bale, T. 2010. *The Conservatives from Thatcher to Cameron*. Cambridge: Polity.

Bale, T. 2012. *The Conservative Party since 1945: The Drivers of Party Change*. Oxford: Oxford University Press.

Barwell, G. 2022. "The last few weeks have damaged the UK and the reputation of the Conservative party". *The Observer*, 2 October.

BBC 1993. *Thatcher: The Downing Street Years*. Episode 4, "Wielding the Knife". Producer, Denys Blakeway. BBC 1, first broadcast 10 November.

BBC 2019a. *Thatcher: A Very British Revolution*. Episode 1, "Making Margaret". Executive producer, Steve Condie; Director, James House. BBC 2, first broadcast 20 May.

BBC 2019b. *Thatcher: A Very British Revolution*. Episode 4, "Downfall". Executive producer, Steve Condie; Director, James House. BBC 2, first broadcast 17 June.

BBC News (online) 2011. "The Specials: How Ghost Town defined an era". BBC News, 17 June

BBC News (online) 2016. "'Useless' bureaucracy hitting teacher morale – union". BBC News, 4 April.

BBC News (online) 2021. "'Greed' and 'capitalism' helped UK's vaccines success, says PM". BBC News, 24 March.

BBC Radio 4 1978. *Desert Island Discs*, 1 February. Transcript available from TF under "Speeches, Interviews & Other Statements".

Bechhofer, F. & B. Elliott 1981. "Petty property: the survival of a moral economy". In F. Bechhofer & B. Elliott (eds), *The Petit Bourgeoisie: Comparative Studies of the Uneasy Stratum*, 182–200. Basingstoke: Macmillan.

Beckett, A. 2009. *When the Lights Went Out: What Really Happened to Britain in the Seventies*. London: Faber.

Biddiss, M. 1987. "Thatcherism: concept and interpretations". In K. Minogue & M. Biddiss (eds), *Thatcherism: Personality and Politics*, 1–20. Basingstoke: Macmillan.

Biffen, J. 1977. "The elephant trap". *Conservative Monthly News*, April.

Biffen, J. 2013. *Semi-Detached*. London: Biteback.

Blond, P. 2010. *Red Tory: How Left and Right have Broken Britain and How we can Fix It*. London: Faber.

Boyson, R. 1971. "Farewell to paternalism". In R. Boyson (ed.), *Down with the Poor: An Analysis of the Failure of the 'Welfare State' and a Plan to End Poverty*, 1–9. London: Churchill Press.

Brittan, S. 1975a. "The economic contradictions of democracy". *British Journal of Political Science* 5(2): 129–59.

Brittan, S. 1975b. *The Economic Consequences of Democracy*. London: Temple Smith.

Brittan, S. 1983. *The Role and Limits of Government: Essays in Political Economy*. London: Temple Smith.

Bruce-Gardyne, J. 1974. *Whatever Happened to the Quiet Revolution?* London: Charles Knight.

Buchanan, J. & G. Tullock 1962. *The Calculus of Consent: Legal Foundations of Constitutional Democracy*. Ann Arbor, MI: University of Michigan Press.

Burke, E. 2004 [1790]. *Reflections on the Revolution in France*. London: Penguin Classics.

Burns, C. 2008. "Margaret Thatcher's greatest achievement: New Labour". Conservativehome, 11 April.

Burton-Cartledge, P. 2021. *Falling Down: The Conservative Party and the Decline of Tory Britain*. London: Verso.

Campbell, J. 1993. *Edward Heath: A Biography*. London: Jonathan Cape.

Campbell, J. 2000. *Margaret Thatcher, Volume One: The Grocer's Daughter*. London: Jonathan Cape.

Campbell, J. 2015. "Margaret Thatcher". In C. Clarke *et al.* (eds), *British Conservative Leaders*, 319–32. London: Biteback.

Charteris-Black, J. 2005. *Politicians and Rhetoric: The Persuasive Power of Metaphor*. Basingstoke: Palgrave Macmillan.

Clarke, K. 2016. *Kind of Blue: A Political Memoir*. London: Macmillan.

Coates, D. 1980. *Labour in Power? A Study of the Labour Government, 1974–1979*. Harlow: Longman.

Cockett, R. 1995. *Thinking the Unthinkable: Think-Tanks and the Economic Counter-Revolution, 1931–1983*. London: Fontana.

Connell, B. 1975. "Margaret Thatcher – A Times profile". *The Times*, 19 May.

Conservative Party 1979. *The General Election Manifesto 1979*. London: Conservative Central Office.

Cowley, P. & M. Bailey 2000. "Peasants' uprising or religious war? Re-examining the 1975 Conservative leadership contest". *British Journal of Political Science* 30(4): 599–629.

Cowling, M. 1990. *Mill and Liberalism*. Second edition. Cambridge: Cambridge University Press.

Criddle, B. 1994. "Members of Parliament". In A. Seldon & S. Ball (eds), *Conservative Century: The Conservative Party since 1900*, 145–68. Oxford: Oxford University Press.

Crines, A., T. Heppell & P. Dorey 2016. *The Political Rhetoric and Oratory of Margaret Thatcher*. Basingstoke: Palgrave Macmillan.

Critchley, J. 1978. "How to get on in the Tory Party". *Political Quarterly* 49(4): 467–73.

Critchley, J. 1985. *Westminster Blues*. London: Elm Tree Books.

Critchley, J. & M. Halcrow 1998. *Collapse of the Stout Party: Decline and Fall of the Tories*. London: Gollancz.

Desai, R. 1994. "'Second-hand dealers in ideas': think tanks and Thatcherite hegemony". *New Left Review* 203 (Jan–Feb): 27–64.

Dorey, P. 2001. *Wage Politics in Britain: The Rise and Fall of Incomes Policy since 1945*. Brighton: Sussex Academic Press.

Dorey, P. 2003. "Margaret Thatcher's taming of the trade unions". In S. Pugliese (ed.), *The Political Legacy of Margaret Thatcher*, 71–85. London: Politico's.

Dorey, P. 2007. "A new direction or another false dawn? David Cameron and the crisis of British Conservatism". *British Politics* 2(2): 137–66.

Dorey, P. 2010a. *British Conservatism: The Politics and Philosophy of Inequality*. London: I. B. Tauris.

Dorey, P. 2010b. "A poverty of imagination: blaming the poor for inequality". *Political Quarterly* 81(3): 333–43.

Dorey, P. 2011. "'A rather novel constitutional experiment': the formation of the 1977–8 'Lib-Lab Pact'". *Parliamentary History* 30(3): 374–94.

Dorey, P. 2013. "'It was just like arming to face the threat of Hitler in the late 1930s': the Ridley Report and the Conservative Party's preparations for the 1984–85 miners' strike". *Historical Studies in Industrial Relations* 34: 173–214.

Dorey, P. 2014. "The stepping-stones programme: the Conservative Party's struggle to develop a trade-union policy, 1975–79". *Historical Studies in Industrial Relations* 35: 89–116.

Dorey, P. 2015a. "The oratory of Margaret Thatcher". In R. Hayton & A. Crines (eds), *Conservative Orators from Baldwin to Cameron*, 103–20. Manchester: Manchester University Press.

Dorey, P. 2015b. "A farewell to alms: Thatcherism's legacy of inequality". *British Politics* 10(1): 79–98.

Dorey, P. 2016a. "'Should I stay or should I go?': James Callaghan's decision not to call an autumn 1978 general election". *British Politics* 11(1): 95–118.

Dorey, P. 2016b. "Weakening the trade unions, one step at a time: the Thatcher governments' strategy for the reform of trade union law, 1979–1984". *Historical Studies in Industrial Relations* 37: 169–200.

Dorey, P. 2016c. "Policies under Cameron: modernisation abandoned". In G. Peele & J. Francis (eds), *David Cameron and Conservative Renewal: The Limits of Modernisation?* 58–81. Manchester: Manchester University Press.

Dorey, P. 2017. "Towards exit from the EU: The Conservative Party's increasing Euroscepticism since the 1980s". *Politics and Governance* 5(2): 27–40.

Dorey, P. 2022. "Neoliberalism in Britain: from origins to orthodoxy". In N. Levy *et al.* (eds), *The Anglo-American Model of Neo-Liberalism and its Consequences*. London: Routledge.

Dorey, P. 2023. "Theresa May's mode of Conservatism: "soft" One Nation Toryism". In A. Crines & D. Jeffery (eds), *Theresa May and Her Legacy*. Basingstoke: Palgrave Macmillan.

Dorey, P. & M. Garnett 2012. "'No such thing as the 'Big Society'? The Conservative Party's unnecessary search for 'narrative' in the 2010 general election". *British Politics* 7(4): 389–417.

Dorey, P. & M. Garnett 2015. "'The weaker-willed, the craven-hearted': The decline of One Nation Conservatism". *Global Discourse* 5(1): 69–91.

Dorey, P. & M. Garnett 2016. *The British Coalition Government, 2010–2015: A Marriage of Inconvenience*. Basingstoke: Palgrave Macmillan.

Dorling, D. 2018. *Peak Inequality: Britain's Ticking Time Bomb*. Bristol: Policy Press.

Drury, C. 2022. "'By November, it's a ghost town': Whitby votes to limit second home sales". *The Independent*, 14 June.

Ellson, A. 2022. "Brighton moves to deter interest in second homes". *The Times*, 22 June.

Fisher, N. 1977. *The Tory Leaders*. London: Weidenfeld & Nicolson.

Fowler, N. 1991. *Ministers Decide*. London: Chapmans.

Friedman, M. 1962. *Capitalism and Freedom*. Chicago, IL: University of Chicago Press.

Friedman, M. 1982. *Capitalism and Freedom*. 20th anniversary edition. Chicago, IL: University of Chicago Press.

Friedman, M. & R. Friedman 1980. *Free to Choose*. Harmondsworth: Penguin.

Gamble, A. 1988. *The Free Economy and the Strong State*. Basingstoke: Macmillan.

Garnett, M. 2004. *The Snake that Swallowed Its Tail: Some Contradictions in Modern Liberalism*. Exeter: Imprint Academic.

Garnett, M. & I. Gilmour 1996. "Thatcherism and the Conservative tradition". In M. Francis & I. Zweiniger-Bargielowska (eds), *The Conservatives and British Society 1880–1990*, 78–93. Cardiff: University of Wales Press.

George, S. 1998. *An Awkward Partner: Britain in the European Community*. Third edition. Oxford: Oxford University Press.

Gilmour, I. 1978. *Inside Right: A Study of Conservatism*. London: Quartet.

Gilmour, I. 1983. *Britain Can Work*. Oxford: Martin Robertson.

Gilmour, I. 1992. *Dancing with Dogma: Britain under Thatcherism*. London: Simon & Schuster.

Goodman, A., P. Johnson & S. Webb (eds) 1997. *Inequality in the UK*. Oxford: Oxford University Press.

Granada TV 1975. *World in Action*, 31 January. Transcript available from The Thatcher Foundation, under "Speeches, Interviews & Other Statements".

Gray, J. 1994. *The Undoing of Conservatism*. London: Social Market Foundation.

Guardian 2013. "Boris Johnson invokes Thatcher spirit with greed is good speech". *The Guardian*, 27 November.

Guardian 2022a. "44% of teachers in England plan to quit within five years". *The Guardian*, 11 April.

Guardian 2022b. "Half of UK adults think young people spend too much to buy a home". *The Guardian*, 13 June.

Halcrow, M. 1989. *Keith Joseph: A Single Mind*. London: Macmillan.

Halfron, R. 2022. "Tories must be the party of compassion". *The Times*, 15 October.

Harris, M. 1996. "The Centre for Policy Studies: the paradoxes of power". In M. Kandiah & A. Seldon (eds), *Ideas and Think Tanks in Contemporary Britain, Volume 2*, 51–64. London: Frank Cass.

Harrison, B. 1994. "Mrs Thatcher and the intellectuals". *Twentieth Century British History* 5(2): 206–45.

Hay, C. 1996. "Narrating crisis: the discursive construction of the 'Winter of Discontent'". *Sociology* 30(2): 253–77.

Hayek, F. 1944. *The Road to Serfdom*. London: Routledge.

Hayek, F. 1976. *Law, Legislation and Liberty, Volume 2: The Mirage of Social Justice*. London: Routledge & Kegan Paul.

Hayek, F. 1988. "The weasel word 'Social'". In R. Scruton (ed.), *Conservative Thoughts: Essays from The Salisbury Review*, 49–54. London: Claridge.

Healey, D. 1990. *The Time of My Life*. Harmondsworth: Penguin.

Heath, E. 1998. *The Course of My Life: My Autobiography*. London: Hodder & Stoughton.

Hennessy, P. 1986. *Cabinet*. Oxford: Blackwell.

Hennessy, P. 2001. *The Prime Minister: The Office and its Holders since 1945*. London: Penguin.

Heppell, T. 2013. "Cameron and Liberal Conservatism: attitudes within the Parliamentary Conservative Party and Conservative ministers". *British Journal of Politics & International Relations* 15(3): 340–61.

Heppell, T. 2014. *The Tories: From Winston Churchill to David Cameron*. London: Bloomsbury.

Heppell, T. 2020. "The ideological composition of the Parliamentary Conservative Party from Thatcher to May". In A. Mullen, S. Farrall & D. Jeffery (eds), *Thatcherism in the 21st Century: The Social and Cultural Legacy*, 15–34. Basingstoke: Palgrave Macmillan.

Heppell, T. & M. Hill 2009. "Transcending Thatcherism? Ideology and the Conservative Party leadership mandate of David Cameron". *Political Quarterly* 80(3): 388–99.

Heseltine, M. 2000. *Life in the Jungle: My Autobiography*. London: Hodder & Stoughton.

HM Treasury 1990. *Privatisations in the United Kingdom: Background Briefing*. London: HM Treasury.

Hogg, S. & J. Hill 1995. *Too Close to Call: Power and Politics – John Major in No. 10*. London: Little, Brown.

Hoskyns, J. 2000. *Just in Time: Inside the Thatcher Revolution*. London: Aurum.

Hotchin, B. 2022. "Second homes owners braced for 300 per cent council tax rise". *The Western Telegraph*, 2 March.

Howe, G. 1994. *Conflict of Loyalty*. London: Macmillan.

Howe, G. *et al.* 1977. *The Right Approach to the Economy.* London: Conservative Central Office.

Hurd, D. 2003. *Memoirs.* London: Little, Brown.

Hutber, P. 1977. *The Decline and Fall of the Middle Class and How it Can Fight Back.* Harmondsworth: Penguin.

Hymas, C. 2019. "Suffocating bureaucracy is wasting police time, Home Office admits". *Daily Telegraph,* 9 July.

Ingham, B. 1991. *Kill The Messenger.* London: HarperCollins.

Ipsos MORI 2013. "Margaret Thatcher (1925–2013)". 8 April.

Jackson, B. 2012. "The think-tank archipelago: Thatcherism and neoliberalism". In B. Jackson & R. Saunders (eds), *Making Thatcher's Britain,* 43–61. Cambridge: Cambridge University Press.

Jackson, B. & R. Saunders 2012. "Introduction: varieties of Thatcherism". In B. Jackson & R. Saunders (eds), *Making Thatcher's Britain,* 1–21. Cambridge: Cambridge University Press.

Jenkins, P. 1989. *Mrs Thatcher's Revolution: Ending of the Socialist Era.* London: Jonathan Cape.

Jenkins, S. 1995. *Accountable to None: The Tory Nationalization of Britain.* London: Hamish Hamilton.

Jordan, G. & J. Richardson 1982. "The British policy style, or the logic of negotiation?" In J. Richardson (ed.), *Policy Styles in Western Europe,* 80–110. London: Allen & Unwin.

Joseph, K. 1975. *Reversing the Trend: A Critical Re-appraisal of Conservative Economic and Social Policies.* Chichester: Barry Rose.

Joseph, K. 1976. *Stranded on the Middle Ground.* London: Centre for Policy Studies.

Joseph, K. 1987. "Escaping the chrysalis of statism: interview with Anthony Seldon". *Contemporary Record* 1(1): 26–31.

Joseph, K. & J. Sumption 1979. *Equality.* London: John Murray.

Judge, D. 2005. *Political Institutions in the United Kingdom.* Oxford: Oxford University Press.

Kavanagh, D. 1987. *Thatcherism and British Politics: The End of Consensus?* Oxford: Oxford University Press.

Kavanagh, D. & A. Seldon 2000. *The Powers Behind the Prime Minister: The Hidden Influence of Number Ten.* London: HarperCollins.

King, A. 1975. "Overload: problems of governing in the 1970s". *Political Studies* 23(2/3): 284–96.

King, A. 1985. "Margret Thatcher: the style of a prime minister". In A. King (ed.), *The British Prime Minister.* Second edition, 96–140. Basingstoke: Macmillan.

King, R. & N. Nugent (eds) 1979. *Respectable Rebels: Middle Class Campaigns in Britain since the 1970s.* London: Hodder & Stoughton.

Kingdon, J. 1984. *Agendas, Alternatives and Public Policies.* Boston, MA: Little, Brown.

Kirkup, J. 2015. *The Lib–Lab Pact: A Parliamentary Agreement, 1977–78.* Basingstoke: Palgrave Macmillan.

Klein, N. 2007. *The Shock Doctrine: The Rise of Disaster Capitalism.* London: Allen Lane.

Krugman, P. 2012. "The austerity agenda". *New York Times,* 31 May.

Kwarteng, K. *et al.* 2012. *Britannia Unchained: Global Lessons for Growth and Prosperity.* Basingstoke: Palgrave Macmillan.

Le Grand, J. 2003. *Motivation, Agency, and Public Policy: Of Knights and Knaves, Pawns and Queens.* Oxford: Oxford University Press.

Lee, R. 2012. *Public Choice, Past and Present: The Legacy of James M. Buchanan & Gordon Tullock*. Dallas: Springer.

Lawson, N. 1992. *The View from No.11: Memoirs of a Tory Radical*. London: Bantam.

Lawson, Lord (Nigel) & Lord (Robert) Armstrong 1994. "Cabinet government in the Thatcher Years". *Contemporary Record* 8(3): 440–52.

Letwin, S. 1992. *The Anatomy of Thatcherism*. London: Fontana.

Lipset, M. 1959. "Democracy and working-class authoritarianism". *American Sociological Review* 24(4): 482–501.

Lipset, M. 1960. *Political Man: The Social Bases of Politics*. New York: Doubleday.

Lipsey, D. 2012. *In the Corridors of Power: An Autobiography*. London: Biteback.

Loewenstein, A. 2015. *Disaster Capitalism: Making a Killing Out of Catastrophe*. London: Verso.

Lopez, T. 2014. *The Winter of Discontent: Myth, Memory, and History*. Liverpool: Liverpool University Press.

Macmillan, H. 1938. *The Middle Way: A Study of the Problems of Economic and Social Progress in a Free and Democratic Society*. London: Macmillan.

Major, J. 1992. *The Next Phase of Conservatism: The Privatisation of Choice*. London: Conservative Political Centre.

Major, J. 1993. *Conservatism in the 1990s: Our Common Purpose*. London: Conservative Political Centre.

Major, J. 1999. *The Autobiography*. London: HarperCollins.

Markeson, S. 2012. "Obituary: Sir Rhodes Boyson". *The Times*, 30 August.

Marsh, D. & R. Rhodes 1992. *Policy Networks in British Government*. Oxford: Clarendon Press.

Matthews-King, A. 2018. "Nurses made to 'choose between paperwork and patient care' because of staff shortages, RCN warns". *The Independent*, 13 May.

May, T. 2017. "The Shared Society". Speech to the Charity Commission, 9 January.

Meyer, A. 1990. *Stand Up and Be Counted*. London: Heinemann.

Miliband, R. 1972. *Parliamentary Socialism: A Study in the Politics of Labour*. London: Merlin.

Millar, R. 1993. *A View from The Wings*. London: Weidenfeld & Nicolson.

Mirowski, P. 2014. *Never Let a Serious Crisis Go to Waste: How Neoliberalism Survived the Financial Meltdown*. London: Verso.

Montgomery, H. 2011. "'Ghost Town': The song that defined an era turns 30". *The Independent*, 3 July.

Montgomery-Massingberd, H. 1986. "Top and bottom of the Tory class". *The Spectator*, 3 May.

Monypenny, W. & G. Buckle 1929. *The Life of Benjamin Disraeli: Volume 2, 1860–1881*. London: Peter Davies.

Moore, C. 2013. *Margaret Thatcher: The Authorized Biography, Vol. 1: Not for Turning*. London: Allen Lane.

Moran, M. 2003. *The British Regulatory State: High Modernism and Hyper-Innovation*. Oxford: Oxford University Press.

Moss, R. 1978. "The defence of freedom". In K. Watkins (ed.), *In Defence of Freedom*, 138–54. London: Cassell.

Mount, F. 2008. *Cold Cream: My Early Life and Other Mistakes*. London: Bloomsbury.

Mount, F. 2012. *The New Few: Power and Inequality in Britain Now*. London: Simon & Schuster.

Niskanen, W. 1971. *Bureaucracy and Representative Government*. Chicago. IL: Aldine, Atherton.

Norton, P. 1978. *Conservative Dissidents: Dissent Within the Parliamentary Conservative Party, 1970–74*. London: Temple Smith.

Norton, P. 1987. "Mrs Thatcher and the Conservative Party: another institution 'handbagged'?" In K. Minogue & M. Biddiss (eds), *Thatcherism: Personality and Politics*, 21–37. Basingstoke: Macmillan.

Norton, P. 1990. "'The lady's not for turning', but what about the rest? Margaret Thatcher and the Conservative Party 1979–89". *Parliamentary Affairs* 43(1): 41–58.

Oakeshott, M. 1967. *Rationalism in Politics and Other Essays*. London: Methuen.

Pack, M. n.d. PollBase: Polls since 1943. Dataset. https://www.markpack.org.uk/opinion-polls/.

Parkinson, C. 1992. *Right at the Centre: An Autobiography*. London: Weidenfeld & Nicolson.

Patten, C. 1983. *The Tory Case*. Harlow: Longman.

Patten, C. 2009. "The Thatcher years". In A. Cooke (ed.), *Tory Policy-Making: The Conservative Research Department 1929–2009*, 79–93. London: Conservative Research Department.

Patten, C. 2018. *First Confession: A Sort of Memoir*. London: Penguin.

Patten, J. 1995. *Things to Come*. London: Sinclair-Stevenson.

Pirie, M. 2012. *Think Tank: The Story of the Adam Smith Institute*. London: Biteback.

Porter, A. 2008. "Tory MPs 'still overwhelmingly Thatcherite'". *Daily Telegraph*, 25 June.

Powell, E. 1969. *Freedom and Reality*. Tadworth: Elliot Right Way Books.

Power, M. 1997. *The Audit Society: Rituals of Verification*. Oxford: Oxford University Press.

Price, D. 1977. "Whither Labour's social contract?". *Tory Challenge*, June.

Prior, J. 1986. *A Balance of Power*. London: Hamish Hamilton.

Pym, F. 1985. *The Politics of Consent*. London: Sphere.

Ranelagh, J. 1992. *Thatcher's People: An Insider's Account of the Politics, the Power and the Personalities*. London: Fontana.

Redwood, J. 1999. *The Death of Britain? The UK's Constitutional Crisis*. Basingstoke: Macmillan.

Renton, T. 2004. *Chief Whip: People, Power and Patronage in Westminster*. London: Politico's.

Rhodes, W. 1997 *Understanding Governance*. Buckingham: Open University Press.

Riddell, P. 1983. *The Thatcher Government*. Oxford: Blackwell.

Ridley, N. 1974. "Why the Tories must break out of a make-believe world". *The Times*, 30 December.

Ridley, N. 1976. "Against incomes policy". *The Spectator*, 27 March.

Ridley, N. 1990. "Interview with Dominic Lawson". *The Spectator*, 14 July.

Ridley, N. 1991. *My Style of Government: The Thatcher Years*. London: Hutchinson.

Rifkind, M. 2016. *Power and Pragmatism: The Memoirs of Malcolm Rifkind*. London: Biteback.

Rogers, S. 2013. "UK public spending since 1963". *The Guardian*, 18 March.

Sanders, D. *et al.* 1987. "Government popularity and the Falklands War: a reassessment". *British Journal of Political Science* 17(3): 281–313.

Scruton, R. 1994. *The Meaning of Conservatism*. Second edition. Basingstoke: Macmillan.

Seldon, A. 1996. "Ideas are not enough". In D. Marquand & A. Seldon (eds), *The Ideas That Shaped Post-War Britain*, 257–89. London: Fontana.

Seldon, A. 2021. *The Impossible Office? The History of the British Prime Minister*. Cambridge: Cambridge University Press.

Seldon, Arthur 1981. *The Emerging Consensus? The First 25 Year of the IEA*. London: Institute of Economic Affairs.

Shepherd, R. 1991. *The Power Brokers: The Tory Party and its Leaders*. London: Hutchinson.

Sherman, A. 2005. *Paradoxes of Power: Reflections on the Thatcher Interlude*. Edited by M. Garnett. Exeter: Imprint Academic.

Shilliam, R. 2018. *Race and the Undeserving Poor*. Newcastle upon Tyne: Agenda.

Slocock, C. 2018. *People Like Us: Margaret Thatcher and Me*. London: Biteback.

Smith, A. 1986 [1776]. *The Wealth of Nations*. Harmondsworth: Penguin Classics.

Smith, M. 1999. *The Core Executive in Britain*. Basingstoke: Macmillan.

Sommerlad, J. 2018. "Section 28: what was Margaret Thatcher's controversial law and how did it affect the lives of LGBT+ people?" *The Independent*, 25 May.

Stacey, E. 2021. "The Conservative Party leadership election of 1975". In A. Roe-Crines & T. Heppell (eds), *Policies and Politics Under Prime Minister Edward Heath*, 377–97. Basingstoke: Palgrave Macmillan.

Syal, R. 2022. "Rishi Sunak admits taking money from deprived areas". *The Guardian*, 5 August.

Tebbit, N. 1988. *Upwardly Mobile*. London: Weidenfeld & Nicolson.

Tebbit, N. 1991. *Unfinished Business*. London: Weidenfeld & Nicolson.

Thatcher, M. 1975. "My kind of Tory Party". *Daily Telegraph*, 30 January.

Thatcher, M. 1979. "Interview with Kenneth Harris". *The Observer*, 25 February.

Thatcher, M. 1980. "A message from the Prime Minister to Oxford University Conservative Association". *Forum* [magazine of the OUCA], August.

Thatcher, M. 1993. *The Downing Street Years*. London: HarperCollins.

Thatcher, M. 1995. *The Path to Power*. London: HarperCollins.

Times 2022. "Need to build affordable homes could be relaxed in planning reforms". *The Times*, 11 October.

Thompson, E. 1980. *Writing by Candlelight*. London: Merlin.

Travers, M. 2007. *The New Bureaucracy: Quality Assurance and its Critics*. Bristol: Policy Press.

Tullock, G., A. Seldon & G. Brady 2000. *Government: Whose Obedient Servant? A Primer in Public Choice*. London: Institute of Economic Affairs.

Waddington, D. 2012. *Memoirs: Dispatches from Margaret Thatcher's Last Home Secretary*. London: Biteback.

Wakefield, L. & P. Kelleher 2021. "The terrible, brutal history of Margaret Thatcher's homophobic Section 28". *PinkNews*, 18 November.

Waldergrave, W. 2022. "The uncertain future of the Tory party". *New Statesman*, 2 November.

Walker, P. 1991. *Staying Power: An Autobiography*. London: Bloomsbury.

Wapshott, N. & G. Brock 1983. *Thatcher*. London: Futura.

Watkins, A. 1991. *A Very Conservative Coup: The Fall of Margaret Thatcher*. London: Duckworth.

Webber, A. 2018. "London firms struggle to recruit because of housing crisis". *Personnel Today*, 26 April.

Whitelaw, W. 1989. *The Whitelaw Memoirs*. London: Aurum.

Wickham-Jones, M. 1997. "Right turn: a revisionist account of the 1975 Conservative Party leadership election". *Twentieth Century British History* 8(1): 74–89.

Willetts, D. 1987. "The role of the prime minister's policy unit". *Public Administration* 65(4): 443–54.

Williams, S. 2010. *Climbing the Bookshelves*. London: Virago.

Wood, J. (ed.) 1965. *A Nation Not Afraid: The Thinking of Enoch Powell*. London: Batsford.

Worsthorne, P. 1978. "Too much freedom". In M. Cowling (ed.), *Conservative Essays*, 141–54. London: Cassell.

Wright, N. 2001. "Leadership, 'bastard leadership' and managerialism: confronting twin paradoxes in the Blair education project". *Educational Management & Administration* 29(3): 275–90.

Yong, B. & R. Hazell 2014. *Special Advisers: Who They Are, What They Do and Why They Matter*. Oxford: Hart.

York, M. 2022a. "What if we banned all second homes?" *Sunday Times*, 19 June.

York, M. 2022b. "Flat-share in the capital too expensive for nurses". *The Times*, 27 August.

Young, H. 1990. *One of Us*. London: Pan.

Young, H. & A. Sloman 1986. *The Thatcher Phenomenon*. London: BBC.

Young, J. 2000. *Britain and European Unity, 1945–1999*. Basingstoke: Palgrave.

Index